ESSAYS IN MORALITY AND ETHICS

Essays in Morality and Ethics

*The Annual Publication
of the College Theology Society*

**Edited by
James Gaffney**

PAULIST PRESS
New York/Ramsey

Library of Congress
Catalog Card Number: 80-80578

ISBN: 0-8091-2248-0

Published by Paulist Press
Editorial Office: 1865 Broadway, New York, N.Y. 10023
Business Office: 545 Island Road, Ramsey, N.J. 07446

Printed and bound in the
United States of America

Contents

Introduction 1

The Other Face of Evil 3
    S. Youree Watson, S.J.

Ethos and Ethics in the New Testament 29
    Leander E. Keck

The Foundations of Paul's Ethics 50
    Al Hiebert

The Zen of Ethics 63
    Silvio E. Fittipaldi

Benevolence: Confucian Ethics and Ecstasy 76
    Thaddeus J. Gurdak

Applying Comparative Ethics
to Multinational Corporations............................. 85
    Roderick Hindery

Theological Guidance for
Moral Development Research 106
    Paul J. Philibert

Beyond Hunger: Toward a Food First Ethic 126
    William J. Wood

Methodological Issues in
the Ethics of Human Sexuality 148
    Luke Salm

Play as an Ethical Paradigm
for Sexual Intercourse 162
    Mary Lou Grad

ESSAYS IN MORALITY AND ETHICS

Introduction

Preparatory arrangements for the twenty-fourth annual meeting of the College Theology Society, held in 1978 at the University of Windsor, Ontario, included the recommendation to participants of a common emphasis on matters having notable relevance to ethics. As a result, many of the presentations and discussions that took place during that meeting assumed ethical perspectives, in at least a secondary way, while treating a great diversity of subjects. Accordingly, it seemed appropriate for the same perspective to be adopted as a principle of selection in compiling the Society's annual publication, which has traditionally organized its contents around some topical theme or academic subspecialty. The present volume is the result, a sampling of "essays in morality and ethics" presented to the College Theology Society, most of which were heard and discussed at its Windsor meeting.

Only a few of the following essays are the work of scholars who would locate their main academic specialty within the field of ethics. Consequently, most of the authors address themselves to specific areas of morality or ethics that have impinged forcefully on their more habitual fields of interest, widely distributed among the theoretical, historical, and practical subdivisions of religious studies.

To specialists in ethics, writings of this kind can appear dilettantish and may be regarded coolly as amateur invasions of a professional terrain. And it can scarcely be denied that, among religious writers, ethical issues are often treated with a nonchalance and concluded with a naiveté that exasperate scholars less superficially acquainted with the history of ethical problems and concepts. But it is also undeniable that, as it exists currently in the English-speaking world, the academic specialty of ethics occasions as much exasperation as it endures.

For people generally continue to suppose that specialists in ethics should have something enlightening to say about what is right and wrong or good and evil in the values and activities of persons

1

and societies. They suppose that ethics offers lessons in morality, and that one who claims expertness in ethics must be, in at least some degree, a moralist. They are disconcerted at finding that a great many of those who call themselves ethicists profess no special interest and claim no special skill at coping with moral issues or expounding moral ideals. They are perplexed to find that what ethicists mainly talk about is—talking about ethics!—and that as a result they talk mostly to one another and have surprisingly little to say in their specialist capacity to anybody else.

Regardless of how one evaluates the progressive narrowing of philosophical attention paid to ethics, one cannot fail to observe that whereas philosophers seldom any longer see moralizing as part of the business of ethics, the demand for moralizing, and for moralists, remains as great as ever. Increasingly, therefore, commentators on morality, as distinct from analysts of ethical discourse, come from other fields than that of philosophy. Among those other fields, religion is conspicuous, and recent years have witnessed ever-increasing interest in moral aspects of nearly all religious studies. The present collection exemplifies attention directed to moral issues by students of religion from a wide variety of viewpoints, theoretical and practical, historical and contemporary. It exemplifies also the interdisciplinary sensitivity typical of modern religious moralizing, which makes increasing use of theories as well as facts derived from secular humanistic and scientific undertakings.

For the publication of these essays, special acknowledgment is owed to Professor Joseph La Barge, of Bucknell University, who organized the Windsor meeting of the College Theology Society; to the Society's president, Professor William Cenkner, of The Catholic University of America; and to Professor Thomas McFadden, of St. Joseph's University, whose skill and energies have for some years guided and encouraged the Society's program of annual publications.

The Other Face of Evil

S. Youree Watson, S.J.

One may well wonder what a philosophical study of the problem of evil is doing in a volume devoted to essays on morality and ethics. A first answer might be that a theodicy or taking up of "the cause of God," that is, an attempt to justify Providence, is nothing less than a reflection on the divine morals from our finite human perspectives and thus the highest branch of moral theology. For God, if not always for his rational creatures, an ethics of consequences seems appropriate, and this is surely not without significance for a more mundane moral theology. Moreover, a good portion of this paper presupposes and to some degree at least seeks to justify, if chiefly by illustration, a hypothesis on the nature of free choice that is directly relevant to any moral theology. Finally, a paper that treats at length of *the* obstacle to right moral behavior, of the source, that is, of all temptation, cannot be judged as wholly irrelevant to a concern with moral action.

While the whole paper is "theological" in a broad understanding of this term, I have added a more narrowly theological Appendix. Granted that it is notably inadequate in itself, it may nevertheless serve the intended purpose of stimulating some strictly theological discussion of what is, as I am sure all will concede, an extremely important matter.

In the middle of the eighteenth century the Berlin Academy offered a prize for the best essay comparing Alexander Pope's position expressed in the *Essay on Man* that "Whatever is is right" with Leibniz's view that this is the best of all possible worlds. Just when the Academy was in process of offering the prize to a certain Adolf Friedrich Theinard, there occurred one of the greatest natural disasters of all times: the Lisbon earthquake. In commenting on this circumstance Yves Congar writes: "Whereupon the whole question

3

took on a wholly new urgency; the simple problem had become a scandal for all the Voltaires of the day. To all those well-meaning mortals who had sought to justify him, it was as though God had replied with the voice of his own thunder: none should justify him, he seemed to say; his will must remain a mystery."[1] We are reminded of God's response to Job and his friends. Who, then, may dare approach the dread problem of evil?

And yet approach it we must, if not without great trepidation, for the problem of evil is *the* problem of believers from the days of Job and Qoheleth down to the present and it will be so in the future despite all our anguished efforts to bring it to bay! The problem of evil is, indeed, a problem only for *believers,* for if there were no God, though the evil would remain, there would no longer be a *problem.* Hume's classic formulation of this problem for believers, derived from the ancients, has had the greatest popularity. He writes: "Epicurus' old questions are yet unanswered. Is he [God] willing to prevent evil, but not able? Then he is impotent. Is he able, but not willing? Then he is malevolent. Is he both able and willing? Whence then is evil?"[2] Hume's import is clear: he is saying that it is not possible to reconcile the existence of God as traditionally conceived with the presence of evil in creation. Of course, it is above all the goodness of God which is at stake. This is why in *J.B.,* Archibald MacLeish's drama about a modern Job, Nickles, the Satan of the play, can reduce Hume to a couplet:

> If God is God, he is not good,
> If God is good, he is not God.

Perhaps we should speak rather of the *mystery* of evil, for it appears to be more a mystery than a problem. Yet it has, I think, problematic aspects that we ought to consider. Moreover, even on mysteries some light may be thrown. Conversely, if rightly approached these may cast light on many other matters. Mindful of Andrew Marvell's fear concerning Milton's endeavor to defend the cause of God in *Paradise Lost*—the fear namely:

> Lest he perplext the things he would explain
> And what was easy he should render vain,[3]

let us approach this question of evil in creation with all reverence and humility. For by a too-facile treatment we should only mock the mystery and intensify the problem.

Evil as Privation

Evil has been traditionally defined as the absence of some due good. It might thus seem to be explained away as something merely negative, in which case evil could appear as some sort of illusion. However, this is not the true implication of the definition. Frederick Copleston remarks: "The description of evil as privation does not diminish the evil in the world, and still less does it do away with it. For the matter of that, if we point out that darkness is not a positive entity like a rock, we do not thereby turn night into day."[4] St. Augustine in his *Confessions,* after asking himself how it can be that evil has crept into a world of good things created by a good God, toys with the thought that perhaps evil does not really exist. But this answer he immediately rejects, saying: "Why, then, do we fear and shun what is not?" And he adds: "If our fear be idle, then this fear itself is evil by which all in vain the heart is tortured."[5]

Though the position that evil is a privation is, I think, only part of the answer to the problem, it needs to be carefully considered. This we cannot do, however, without first distinguishing the principal ways in which the word "evil" and its synonyms are used. To this we must now attend. In its most general sense we may define "evil" as that which is in itself reasonably feared, hated, and as far as possible shunned. This, of course, is just the beginning of a definition, an effort to identify what we are talking about. It immediately gives rise to the questions: *What* is reasonably feared, hated, and shunned? It will be necessary at this point to distinguish two classes of objects that fall under this description. First there are what we may call physical or natural evils, such as illness and death. Then there are moral evils, that is (as we understand the term here) sin and other character failings. Now, in both these kinds of evil there is indeed a privation, an absence of a due good. In the case of a physical evil there may be the lack of some integral part of a being. Thus a tree may be missing a branch that it should have. This would be an evil for it. The tree itself would be a deprived thing (in English we would not call such a tree "evil"; we should say rather that the tree is deficient or defective). There is also the cause of the tree's deprivation, say a hurricane that broke off the limb. This evil we may call the "depriver." Similarly a man (the deprived) may be lacking a foot (the deprivation) because of a hand grenade (instrument of deprivation) thrown in time of war by an enemy (the depriver).

On the other hand the deprivation may be not of a physical part

but of the right order of parts. Every illness is such a deprivation of
the due good of order. Thus pneumonia is an evil in the sense of a
deprivation of the right order in the lungs. This is evil in the primary sense. The person suffering from pneumonia is in a deprived and
hence evil condition. That which caused or conditioned the pneumonia, let us say a cold draft to which the man was long exposed, was
an ill wind that blew him no good, an evil in the sense of that which
deprives another of the order due. From this too brief analysis it
should be clear that involved in every physical evil there is indeed a
deprivation, but that in a broader, very common sense of the word,
positive things too are termed evil, or at least deficient. Such are all
things deprived of any part or of the right order of their parts; and
whatever causes or is in any way responsible for such a deficiency is,
even in English, called evil or bad for that which it deprives of what
is due to it. Thus we think of devastating earthquakes and ship-
wrecking storms, snakes that bite us and wasps that sting us as being so many evils.

What of moral evil? It too may be conceived as primarily a privation or deprivation of the right order in human actions. We com-
monly call this sin, and he who suffers from this deprivation is also
the one who alone can cause this deprivation. In the sinner the depriver and the deprived coincide. *He,* to be sure, is a positive reality,
as is the *act* which is disordered, but that which is the root evil is
not an action as such, much less the person who acts, but rather the
disorder or lack of order in this action being performed by this person in these circumstances, the necessary result of which is the destruction or diminishment of some value. Thus wiggling my finger
is certainly no evil in itself, but will be so if the wiggling moves the
trigger of a gun aimed at an innocent person. In this case it will be
a disordered action, an evil, a sin (formally so, of course, only if the
result was intended).

The Problem of Moral Evil

Evil does seem to be at base a privation of some due good, but
the fundamental problem remains: How can an all-good, all-powerful God allow such deprivations to occur when presumably he could
prevent them? My purpose in this little essay is to offer some
thoughts that may, I hope, give a glimpse at the reasons why. Someone has said that "The Problem of Evil . . . seems to attract bad arguments as jam-making attracts wasps."[6] We must be careful!

Let us first consider moral evil, which is in truth much the greater evil. Joinville, the chronicler at the court of St. Louis IX of France, once wrote in his journal that he would rather commit thirty mortal sins than be afflicted with leprosy. He said this because he was a sinner. St. Louis was of a quite contrary opinion. At his saintly best he would rather have died than commit one mortal sin. And whatever we ourselves might *do* if faced with such an option as Joinville imagined, if we are believers or simply honest-minded individuals, we must judge that not he, but St. Louis had the right idea. Moral evil is more to be shunned than any physical evil. It follows that the problem of evil is here most acute. God is believed to loathe sin and yet he "permits" it.[7]

Our fundamental "explanation" for this must, naturally, be our fundamental "explanation" for God's "permission" of any evil; namely, that this evil is so connected with some greater good, that the latter cannot be realized without the "permission" of the evil or at least—as in the case of moral evil—of the possibility of this. As regards the "permission" of the possibility of moral evil, the great good, the high value in question here is man's free choice of objective worth over merely subjective satisfaction, that is, of duty over sheer pleasure when these two are in conflict. For if a person is to be able freely to choose this particular course of action, he or she must be free also to choose the contrary course; that is, to prefer his subjective satisfaction to objective value, pleasure to duty.

Sometimes it is said that God knows in advance what each man will at every moment choose and so could block any wrong choice and allow only right choices. This seems to me impossible. God cannot know a free choice infallibly until that choice is made, for in truth there is nothing to be known. Hence St. Thomas Aquinas among others held that God knows the free future choices of men only in their occurrence. He holds, to be sure, that God in his eternity, being outside of time, is in his eternal "now" equally present to every moment of time. Even so, there would be no possibility of God's blocking an evil free choice inasmuch as he knows this only in itself, in its actual doing, not through its causes (the chooser himself and his situation just prior to the choice).

Why, then, does God "permit" sin? Because he values so much man's freedom in choosing good, this freedom which, as Dante says, is the Creator's greatest gift to man[8]. St. Augustine, who did not always speak so clearly on human freedom, writes in his treatise *On Free Will*: "Neither the sins nor the misery [consequent upon sin] is necessary to the perfection of the universe, but souls as souls are necessary which have power to sin if they so will, and become miserable if they sin." Souls, I take it, are said to be "necessary" for the perfection of the universe inasmuch as without rational creatures creation would appear pointless[9].

If what I have said above is correct, it follows that those who would make God responsible for sin are in error. They—without realizing it—often assume that man is not really free, that he is, as we say, psychologically determined, and therefore God, knowing perfectly an individual's character at any given moment and the situation in which he finds himself, can without fail know precisely what the man is going to choose at the next moment and so can, if desirable, block that choice. There are, it is true, some believers who, while wishing to acknowledge free will in man, conceive of God's foreknowledge in such a way that they too, in effect, seem to deny human freedom. These must seek a much more complex and, I believe, much less satisfactory answer: God does foresee evil choices in such a way that he could prevent their being made, but nevertheless permits them because from the sin itself he will draw some good. One difficulty with this is that divine omnipotence can surely draw more good from a good choice than it can from an evil choice. There are still other Christian theologians who hold that God as First Cause can bring it about that individuals freely choose whatever he wishes them to choose by determining them to choose this freely. This I simply do not understand. It is as paradoxical as Rousseau's statement that if men in civil society do not want to exercise their freedom, they must be forced to be free. Moreover, such a view seems to make God himself responsible for sin in a way he cannot be. Essential though it certainly is, God's grace must never determine man's choices if these are to be truly free. What God desires above all, it seems, is man's free option of the good, and this would not be achieved by turning man into a moral robot. To put the same in another way, what God desires is to be loved in himself and in his images. Now, although love in its beginnings is spontaneous, it is fostered and grows through attention to the beloved, through purification from the obstacles to loving and through the faithful performance of the works of love, and all of these depend on the free will, and to them is applicable that wise saying of Kierkegaard: "How could it occur to love to wish to use compulsion to be loved?"[10].

The position defended here, though not without its own difficulties, can help us answer not a few objections. For example, one author states: "God is said to be omniscient as well as all-powerful and, therefore, He knew what we would do with our free will and, nevertheless, He created us. The responsibility for this evil is His."[11] This philosopher misses the point. For, as C.S. Lewis has indicated in his *The Problem of Pain,* the reality of a choice, sinful or virtuous, is the choice itself, and what God knows is that actual choice at the moment it is made. To say that God need not have tried the experiment in the Garden of Eden because in his omniscience he must have known that Adam and Eve would make the wrong choice, is to say that because God knows, the thing known by God need not exist![12]

The Problem of Physical Evil

Let us turn now to a consideration of physical evil. The allusion just made to Adam and Eve and to original sin leads us to a consideration of the view that all physical evils in creation stem from original sin and subsequent actual sins. I cannot nor would I wish to refute this opinion, but I confess that it seems to me very improbable. If God has chosen to create an evolving universe, as I believe he has, it seems inevitable that there be in it an enormous amount of physical evil, that is, of beings that are deficient and of beings that must be sooner or later destroyed. For evolution, like all growth, requires a sacrifice of the less perfect for the sake of the more perfect. As the peculiar beauty of the baby gives place to the still greater loveliness of the child, and the particular values associated with childhood slowly disappear with the coming of adolescence and the gradual maturing of the individual into the fullness of manhood or womanhood, so the universe "grows" from the simpler compounds to the more complex, and these in turn lose their independence to become very simple organisms, which themselves yield place to complex organisms that need to utilize the simpler creatures for their survival. These, as the creative advance proceeds, are subordinated to still higher types, until finally we reach man himself, who uses all subhuman things, including all plants and animals when needful, for his own good. It is certain that neither animals nor man could exist without "evil" coming to other organisms, not to mention the breakdown of innumerable splendid molecular formations![13]

But could not God have made a universe in which there would be no sacrifice, no lower values preparing for and giving place to higher values? Doubtless he could, but can we be sure that the sum of values that such a universe would represent would equal that of an evolving universe like our own? I can only say that the organic, dynamic character of this our universe seems to me to surpass in order, in beauty, in being that of any "nonsacrificial" universe of which I can conceive. Thus if there are to be *living* beings, *sensitive* beings, *human* beings—and what a glory is caught and expressed in each of these words!—then there must be constant destruction of lesser values for the sake of higher values; in a word, there must be physical evil. In an enormously complex whole evolving by statistical laws (as, it seems, *must* be the case), there will, of course, be multitudinous cases in which lower values by chance triumph over higher values. But the long-term movement has been upward, ever upward to man. And those who believe that this is the consequence of the divine providential plan, have very good reason indeed to hope that the advance will continue, though with much less certitude since it is now contingent in part on man's own free choices.

John Stuart Mill was so obsessed with the existence of evil in the world that he could not bring himself to hold that God is infinite in power. Yet even he, reflecting on the evolutionary process, made bold to write:

> No one whose opinion deserves a moment's consideration can doubt that most of the great positive evils of the world are in themselves removable, and will, if human affairs continue to improve, be in the end reduced within narrow limits. . . . All the grand sources, in short, of human suffering are in great degree, many of them almost entirely, conquerable by human care and effort; even though their removal is grievously slow—though a long succession of generations will perish in the breach before the conquest is completed, and this world become all that, if will and knowledge were not wanting, it might easily be made—yet every mind sufficiently intelligent and generous to bear a part, however small and inconspicuous, in the endeavour will draw a noble enjoyment from the contest itself, which he would not for any bribe in the form of selfish indulgence consent to be without.[14]

Perfectly applicable here is G. K. Chesterton's famous quip: "Life is a glorious battle, but a miserable truce." If we accept the challenge, make the effort entailed, pain becomes meaningful. Now, as the great psychologist Viktor Frankl tells us, once pain has a meaning, it ceases in a sense to be pain; and he quotes Nietzsche as saying that if only we have a *why* we can put up with almost any *how*.[15]

Since we have all along linked physical evil in creation with the evolutionary character of the universe, it will be appropriate to end this section with a quotation from that contemporary Christian thinker whose name has been most closely associated with this view. In *Comment je vois* Pierre Teilhard de Chardin writes:

> Out of stubborn habit, the Problem of Evil continues to be declared insoluble; this is a sort of reflex action and really one wonders what reason there is for it. In the Cosmos en-visaged by antiquity as issuing ready-made from the hands of the Creator, it was but natural that it should appear dif-ficult to reconcile the existence of a World partially evil and the existence of a God at once good and omnipotent. But from our modern standpoint, with its idea of a uni-verse in a state of cosmogenesis . . . how can anyone fail to see that, intellectually speaking, the famous problem no longer exists?[16]

The Problem of Pain

Pain! In my divisions and subdivisions of evil, I said nothing di-rectly about pain, and yet for most men, pain is the great evil, al-most the only evil. But pain, central as it may be in human consciousness, is in reality inseparable from the more basic evils of sin and physical disorder, for, as a number of psychologists tell us, pain is nothing other than the consciousness, the awareness of dis-order.[17] If there is to be no pain, then either there must be no disor-der or if there is we must be anesthetized in its regard. Always keeping in mind this unbreakable link between pain and the priva-tion of some good, let us proceed to a consideration of evil in the sense of pain, specifically to a reflection on the problem of pain, as it is called. In the last analysis, it is this above all which gives rise to those doubts or temptations to doubt the goodness of God which almost all experience at times. To many it has appeared as it did to Camus "the insurmountable barrier to Christianity."[18]

One dare not speak glibly about pain. Unless one has himself undergone the agonies that have afflicted many of the human race and still afflict them today, he will in his fine discourse about the value of suffering be subject to the blunt charge that he does not know what he is talking about. Especially a philosopher! Shake-speare, we recall, has one of the characters in *Much Ado about Nothing* say:

> For there was never yet philosopher
> that could endure the toothache patiently.[19]

The first thing to remark is that if we say God is good, we can-not in the next breath say that he is indifferent to human suffering. This would be to take away all meaning from the previous state-ment. On the other hand, the goodness of an infinite Being will as-suredly manifest itself in different ways from that of finite beings like ourselves. Because God is omniscient and acts in the light of eternity, he will see things quite differently from us. God, to be sure, always takes the long view, indeed the eternal perspective. But what we cannot admit is that God does not hate evil in itself and, specifically, pain in itself. Hence we must hold that if God per-mits any suffering the reason can only be, as we said at the begin-ning in regard to evil in general, that this suffering is necessarily linked with some greater good, that is, some value of which the pain is either a necessary condition or an inevitable consequence.

How can this be? By way of a beginning let us reflect on the fol-lowing remarks of Ninian Smart:

> A person is praised for generosity because very often there is a conflict of generosity and self-interest. We credit peo-ple with courage on such grounds as that they have faced adverse situations with calm and disregard for danger . . . These examples, then, are meant to indicate that the con-cept *goodness* is applied to beings of a certain sort, beings who are liable to temptations, possess inclinations, have fears, tend to assert themselves, and so forth; and that if they were to be immunized from evil they would have to be built in a different way. But it soon becomes apparent that to rebuild them would mean that the ascription of good-ness would become unintelligible, for the reasons why men are called good and bad have a connection with human na-ture as it is empirically discovered to be. Moral utterance is embedded in the cosmic status quo.[20]

I take Smart to be saying that if we eliminate all pain from the world, we eliminate with it all moral worth, and I quite agree with him. To be sure, one must understand "pain" in the very broadest sense so that it includes whatever is to any degree unpleasant, whatever is not to one's taste, anything that involves unattractive effort however slight, anything that "costs" however little, which in turn includes the foregoing of some pleasure even though trivial (giving up a great pleasure can, of course, be a great pain). Why is pain a condition for moral worth *humanly* understood? Because, as I suggested above, a moral choice is always between a greater objective value and something that while of lesser objective value is more pleasurable or, it may be, less painful. If I choose the former the motive must be the objective value in itself, whereas if I choose the latter the motive must be the greater pleasure, or the lesser pain, which will be experienced by me; in brief, a choice between duty and pleasure when the two are in conflict. Note that one's duty—and this, I should claim, is the first principle of all morality—is to promote objective value to the greatest extent possible in the circumstances. Thus I am morally good when I am seeking to preserve and intensify premoral good (also called ontological good, ontic good—what I have termed objective value). And I submit that if there should be no action even relatively unpleasant (less pleasant than some alternative), there could be no moral choice as we understand this in the case of human beings. If the line of duty always coincided with the most pleasurable course of action, no other choice would be humanly possibly. For freedom of human choice, I should insist, is always between incommensurable alternatives, such as objective value and subjective satisfaction (pleasure); for if we act out of a pure love for duty, we shall always choose the greater objective value, and if out of sheer desire for pleasure, we shall always choose the greater pleasure. If doing one's duty cost nothing, if it were always the most pleasant thing to do, everyone would do his or her duty, but no one would deserve any praise for this, for virtue would be a necessity, lacking that freedom which must ground what we humans recognize as moral worth. The physical (premoral) perfection of the universe would doubtless be increased, but in my opinion this would not compensate for the loss of that peculiar loveliness possible in the free actions of a finite being, namely *moral* splendor.

It may help if at this juncture we try to imagine a world without pain. This, according to Henri de Lubac, would be "an earthly existence undisturbed by struggle or contradiction, without suffering but also without aspiration. . . . A perfectly tranquil world with no room for either saints or heroes!"[21] Similar ideas have been expressed by the late Martin D'Arcy. As he provides us with a number of vivid images illuminating the matter, it will be worthwhile to quote from him at some length. He writes:

> All are half aware that what is best can be won only at great cost, that the unique joy of climbing Everest cannot be had by walking up Ludgate Hill. . . . [Let's try to imagine] what this earthly life would be like without pain, difficulty and danger, so lacklustre in fact as to be infinitely boring. We should have to revise most of our estimates of value. No longer would St. George be an emblem, St. Laurence an inspiration. Heroism would be put out of fashion and the world as dull as a duckpond; for the truth is that above all in the conquest of self, in the discipline of the passions, the endurance of dark nights and in the self-sacrifice for others, the self rises to its proper pitch and is most truly human.[22]

And elsewhere the same philosopher writes:

> If . . . God were to interfere manifestly in our human troubles and guarantee success always to the good, life would become puny and unadventurous. Like Aladdin we should always be able to ensure getting what we want; we should be playing the game of life with marked cards. We dishonour human choices and human life by making it so trivial.[23]

Eloquently said, though I feel that Father D'Arcy overemphasizes the heroic and "adventurous," obscuring somewhat the thing that I myself have insisted upon, namely that pain in the very broad sense defined is the condition not just for heroism, but for *any* moral value here on earth. The American philosopher Josiah Royce states that "The best world for a moral agent is one that needs him to make it better."[24] Good! But I would go even further and say that the *only* world for a moral agent is one that needs him to make it better.

Some Objections

Is not this a case of overkill? Louis Dupré argues:

> If physical evil is really indispensable to moral progress, morality itself becomes a self-defeating process. For it

obliges each man within his means to lessen the amount of physical evil in the world. It exhorts him to eradicate war, famine, disease. Yet think of the wonderful opportunities for the practice of virtue which would be lost if man were ever moral enough to be successful in this struggle.[25]

A serious objection, calling for much reflection. My own basic answer would be to point out that a lesser good is always "evil" in relationship to a higher attainable good, for in the lesser good there is a privation of the higher good for which one should strive. Each person can always improve himself, his character. The hero can become more heroic, the saint more saintly (in truth, the genuine hero *is* the saint). But not without effort, not without pain. So too the world can always be improved, perfected in a thousand ways. But never without effort, never without pain. We must struggle day by day toward the glorious goal envisioned by Teilhard when all men and women on the surface of the globe shall have, as it were, but one mind and one heart, freely yielding to the sweet attraction of Christ, the Omega Point. Then, when this great end has been attained, as we hope it shall, when the painful struggle is over, comes the Parousia!

Will there indeed come a time when all striving will end? Some theologians have suggested that even in heaven there may be something analogous. For example, Friedrich von Hügel has written:

It is not difficult to find, within the deepest characteristics of the human soul even upon earth and the most certain and most dominant conditions of the Other Life, operative causes for the continuance in Heaven itself of the essentials in the nobility furnished by devoted suffering and self-sacrifice here below. . . . It is God, as He is in Himself, and not as He is only partially seen by them, whom these spirits [in Heaven] desire to comprehend, to love, to will and to serve. Hence, even in Heaven, there remains for the saved soul, room and the need to transcend itself, to lose itself, that it may truly find itself.

Von Hügel pictures the soul in heaven as plunging "away from the quite clear yet limited vision, into a wider, but at first dimmer experience of the great Reality." And he adds that "such plunges of the soul there into God, and the somewhat similar goings-out there of the same soul to its fellows . . . are the equivalents of men's heroic plunges here away from sin and self.[26]

Let us return to the objection of Dupré. God, it seems, desires the physical perfecting of the universe. He desires also the moral perfecting of man. More precisely, he desires the physical perfecting of the universe *through* the moral activity and so through the moral perfecting of man. They proceed together, and may reach completion simultaneously at the Parousia, after which part of man's everlasting joy will be the beauty of the City of God to which he and his fellows have contributed through their Christ-united efforts. Not a static object of contemplation, for every least effort made, each pain endured in the building of the City will be, as it were, a stone in that grand edifice—a joy forever! And if, according to the view of Von Hügel and others, a certain amount of construction will continue throughout eternity, the basic truth illustrated remains the same. What God loves is creation. What we should love—and will in the full light of love—is above all the perfecting of the universe through the moral efforts of man, or shall we say, the universe perfected through the moral efforts of man?

Another very serious objection concerns the suffering of children. We recall the moving passage in *The Brothers Karamazov* in which Ivan presents this objection to Alyosha. We may remember also the equally graphic treatment of the problem in Camus's novel *The Plague*. The basic argument is always the same. Suffering is said to be permitted by God because human beings by accepting this as they should can profit morally. But a child, a mere infant, how could it get any good out of this evil?

A first, tentative response might do: Is it altogether certain that there is no incipient capacity for virtue even in an infant? No one surely would claim that a child of, say, two years of age is capable of controlling its feelings to any notable extent. However, it may be that even a baby has at times some slight area of free response that might, for instance, determine the decibels of its screaming. If so then in this narrow, dim area of the infant's consciousness pain could have an element of moral purpose. I myself would not wish to press this line of argument. If I bring it up here, the chief reason is that there is an important analogy in the case of adults. One often hears that pain frequently overwhelms a person, crushes him or her, and in all such instances has a negative, rather than positive, moral value. But there is an oversight here. For even though an individual is overcome by his sorrow and eventually loses all freedom, this does not mean that in the process he did not struggle valiantly. Now, it is this fact that is all-important, not what happened after his total loss of freedom. His virtuous effort, though not achieving its goal of a serene acceptance, persists everlastingly in its contribution to the upbuilding of the City of God. The psychological failure is *relatively* unimportant.

On another plane the suffering of the child is but a part of the total weight of suffering consequent upon a world like ours, a world in evolution. No doubt God could intervene miraculously on each occasion that a child would be on the point of suffering, but it is at least doubtful that such an "unlawful" world would really be a better place for the mass of mankind. Human depravity would doubtless abuse the situation shamelessly.

This is, I believe, the moment to say that for any less inadequate "answer" to the problem of pain, one must presuppose the religious doctrine of eternal life. If this present life were all, we might well wonder why in fact God does not frequently intervene to prevent at least the severer sufferings and those that seem to have less purpose. However, in the light of eternity things look very different. Time is a snap-of-the-fingers compared with everlastingness and this world's worst a pinprick in comparison with the best of the world to come. The child of whom we have been speaking will for all eternity rejoice that his fleeting sufferings gave occasion to others, above all his parents, to exercise compassion and to grow in love. He will not then be the least rebellious at his role of Holy Innocent. This line of argument will, of course, be of no emotional help to unbelieving parents. Nevertheless, it is not, I think, out of place even in a purely philosophical treatment of the problem of pain. For a philosopher offering reasons that seek to explain why God permits evil as he does is surely justified in considering the immortality of the soul, if not strictly demonstrable, at least as a possibility that certainly ought to be taken into account.

A very ancient but really superficial objection against the goodness of God is based upon the fact that it is often the good who suffer, the wicked who prosper. I shall comment on this difficulty by means of a quotation from A. E. Taylor in his work *Does God Exist?* The present objection, Taylor tells us

> rests throughout on the assumption that if there were a God directing the course of events, his purpose *could* only be to make the "good" happy and the "bad" unhappy in respect of their earthly fortunes. But this assumption is wholly arbitrary, and if there is anything in the Christian view that God's purpose is not simply to give the "good" a good time, but to educate His rational creatures into a cer-

tain type of character, it is actually false. All that is proved by the calamities of the "good" and the undeserved successes of the "bad" is that, if there is a divine purpose, it is nothing so crude as remunerating righteousness with worldly felicity.[27]

With these thoughts we may compare Kant's idea that the purpose of earthly life is not to make us happy, but to make us into the sort of persons who will be fit to enjoy a happiness which is yet to come. We may recall also the pregnant saying of Gandhi: "Every moment of my life I realize that God is putting me on trial." He is indeed—it is true for each of us—but the trials, as Gandhi must have known, are so many opportunities not only to manifest our love for value, but to grow in love for this—in the concrete, to grow in love for God and our neighbor—and so we may, with the saints, exult in our "trials." This earth is not so much a vale of tears as a "vale of soul-making." Keats was right on this if not on the rest of his "theodicy." The truth he glimpsed has been caught again by Jean Daniélou in his *The Lord of History*, where he writes:

> The real purpose of history is to achieve—through the mill of temporal vicissitudes—the manufacture and education of human souls. The real measure of history is not to be sought in the level of technical attainment, but in the more or less effective production of personalities, "which represent the highest things we know in the mundane realm."[28]

A last thought on the objection based on the trials of the "good." Wittgenstein, the son of a millionaire, gave his fortune away early in life, and one of the reasons he gave for doing so was that he wished to be loved for himself, not for expected favors. Now, if God were regularly to give earthly rewards to those who serve him, he would all too often be loved only for his blessings. He too wants to be loved for himself!

Argumentum ad Hominem

Quite possibly God might have created a universe in which no creature was ever deficient in anything and so never felt pain. As we have been saying all along, it is by no means evident that this would be a better creation, but however this may be, what I now wish to note is that we would not be part of that other creation. *We are what we are:* these corporeal, sensitive, rational beings. Those differently constituted beings that would inhabit the flawless, painless world we have imagined may be very splendid indeed, but alas they would not be *we!* By the improving of things, the redoing of creation, we have eliminated ourselves. Now, I do not know about others, but personally I am willing to take my share of pain in order to be here. If one holds for the destiny to which as believers we aspire—an everlastingness of joy—the answer could not be in doubt for a single moment. "To be or not to be—that is the question," says Hamlet. *To be,* replies the Christian, and I think the great majority of mankind, even those without the Christian hope, would join him here: *To be—that is the answer.*[29]

A Philosophical Afterword

We shall never, of course, solve all the difficulties connected with the presence of evil in the universe. But if we have weighty reasons for holding that there must be a First Cause and that this First Cause must be all-perfect, and so all-good, all-loving—which, to be sure, I have not attempted to prove here, but have all along assumed, for otherwise the *problem* of evil does not even arise—then the difficulties of which we have spoken are no solid ground for doubting God's goodness, "just as the mysterious conduct of a friend in some matter may perplex me, if I have not the clue to it, but does not disturb my confidence in his honor and integrity, if I have sufficient independent grounds to be assured of them."[30] Moreover, if we add to these strong positive reasons for affirming God's goodness some passing insights into how this operates in the concrete; that is, if we can develop, as we have attempted to do here, certain at least plausible explanations for the permission by God of various kinds of evil, then perhaps the problem of evil, though it defy complete solution, will trouble us less.

We may also take confidence from the fact that according to the eminent humanistic psychologist Abraham Maslow men who reach the higher peaks of human experience see life as good and cease to regard pain as a problem. One of the characteristics of such peak experiences is, he tells us the "transcendence of death, pain, sickness, evil," all these being seen to be "necessary." As Christians, to be sure, we shall be most interested in the testimony of the saints and especially of the mystics among them, and there can be no doubt that this confirms what Maslow says here. They better than anyone understood the "necessity" of physical evils, of suffering, for the growth of love.[31]

A Theological Appendix

The primarily philosophical reasonings in which I have engaged up to now may possibly appear suasive to one who at the moment is not in pain. They would not, I am sure, make much impression on one who is in intense pain. I am reminded of something Raymond J. Nogar says in his *Lord of the Absurd:*

> To a mother whose tiny child has just died of cancer, the suggestion that, in spite of all, the celestial spheres still sing in cosmic harmonies, has the consolation of a mouthful of ashes.[32]

Truly, we must appeal to faith if we are to be convinced that, as St. Paul puts it, "the suffering of this time is as nothing compared with the glory which is to come."[33] Indeed, if we are to be fully reconciled to pain we must turn our eyes to our Savior, who for love of us hangs in agony on the cross. In doing so, of course, we go far beyond the limits of philosophy. But then, none of us—happily—is a *mere* philosopher. And although in speaking of theology strictly so called I am no longer sticking to my academic last, with all the risks that not doing so entails, I feel I must, in fact, end on a properly theological note, and that this is justified inasmuch as those who urge the problem of evil and base objections upon it are, as a rule, attacking not the views of philosophical theists, but those of Christian believers.

Let me begin by remarking that as Claudel says, "Christ did not come to do away with suffering; he did not come to explain it; he came to fill it with his presence."[34] How Christ does this we are told by Louis Evely, who writes: "When his hour had come, the hour of his true revelation, Christ made no more miracles. He died on the cross. He revealed the humanity of God, the weakness of God, the suffering of God, the love of God."[35] The theme of God suffering is a favorite one with Evely. He returns to it elsewhere:

> If the man Christ alone suffers, then say that he alone is Father, that he alone is Love. An impassive Father? Then you had better stop calling him "Father." An insensitive love? Do not say it is "love."

The revelation of God took place in the greatest suffering. Do not correct the revelation according to the taste of your philosophy. If God manifested himself in that way, it is because there was no means of expressing in our human language, in our human flesh (the Word became flesh), what God is, without expressing suffering.[36]

I am well aware that Evely is not a professional theologian, that his orthodoxy in some of his later writings is not unquestioned. Nevertheless, I believe what he says here calls for most careful consideration. No doubt the idea of God suffering cannot be taken univocally, yet it is not *mere* metaphor either. The divine nature cannot be changed in itself, but God's relationships to the world, and here I should include his knowledge and love for his creatures, can and do, I think, change. The divine compassion, revealed in Christ, is of the really real.

Moreover, we know that a number of professional theologians are in accord with Evely's views as expressed here, beginning perhaps with Bonhoeffer, who in his *Letters and Papers from Prison* tells us that "Man is summoned to share in God's sufferings at the hands of the godless world."[37] This idea has caught on, especially it seems, among Liberation theologians. Thus Jon Sobrino writes in his *Christ at the Crossroads:*

People in Latin America, however, seem to feel almost automatically what Dietrich Bonhoeffer expressed in intuitive, poetic terms: "Only a God who suffers can save us." Paradoxical as the statement might seem, we should not relegate it to the realm of pious thinking or rhetoric. It must be analyzed carefully because the very essence of the Christian God is at stake. For Aristotle, God is the thinking process which thinks about itself, but which is apathetic with respect to history. For Saint John, God is love. Is that statement real? ... Is it something more than a mere analogy? ... If our answer to those questions is yes, then we must ask ourselves how God can express that love, his ultimate word to human beings, in a world of misery without himself being affected by that misery.

The problem in talking about God as love is that we must not trivialize this ultimate statement of revelation. So we must insist that love has to be *credible* to human beings in an unredeemed world. That forces us to ask ourselves whether God can really describe himself as love if historical suffering does not affect him. It is not at all self-evident to human beings that suffering because of love is an imperfection, since in our world love passes through suffering.[38]

Subsequently Sobrino cites Moltmann's *Der gekreuzigte Gott* as follows:

If love is the acceptance of another without taking thought for one's own well-being, then it contains within itself the capacity for compassion and the freedom to suffer the otherness of the other. An inability to suffer would contradict the basic Christian assertion that God is love.[39]

The fact that I myself am not a theologian justifies me, I trust, in turning this Appendix into a tissue of quotes. On the present matter of God's suffering I should like to offer one more citation, this time from a review by John Farrelly of Jean Galot's *Dieu souffre-t-il?*, published in Paris in 1976:

Sin ... touches God interiorly, for it wounds or pains the love He has for us, although it does not affect the divine nature, which is impassible. As one human being who loves another is wounded by the other's rejections, so too God suffers from man's sin. G. holds that there is a real analogy between these two cases, since what is essential in the first relation is also found in the second. To suffer does not diminish God's perfection; indeed, He would be inferior if He were not free to take the risks of love that His engagement with free human beings in history constitutes. . . .
Suffering remains a scandal for the world as long as the appearance is given that God asks men and women to suffer when He Himself does not have to bear the cost. Perhaps a development of the theological theme of God's suffering that gives more weight to Scripture's teaching than traditional theology does can help to overcome this scandal and the spirit of revolt that sometimes results from it.[40]

If one is unwilling to go quite so far as some of the writers whom I have quoted here one ought at least to stress the role of the cross in Christianity, never soft-pedaling the sufferings of God-made-Man. It is indeed only through the Incarnation that we can somehow imagine God's sympathy for our sufferings, the love that has led him to share them. One of the three Kings in Dorothy Sayers' nativity play is describing the significance of the Incarnation as he conceives it:

> . . . If only God will not be indifferent,
> If He is beside me, bearing the weight of
> His own creation.
> If I may hear His voice among the voices
> of the vanquished,
> If I may feel His hand touch mine in the darkness,
> If I may look upon the hidden face of God
> And read in the eyes of God
> That He is acquainted with grief.

And, of course, the speaker's wish is fulfilled in marvelous fashion![41]

I referred above to the famous conversation between Ivan and Alyosha in Dostoevsky's *The Brothers Karamazov*. Toward the end Ivan says to his brother: "Listen, I took the case of children only to make my case clearer. Of the other tears of humanity with which the earth is soaked from its crust to its centre, I will say nothing."[42] Yes, truly, the earth is soaked with tears, but mingled with those tears of humanity are the tears of God, the tears of one divine as well as human. If God as God cannot suffer, perhaps he becomes man so that he can do so. Simone Weil writes in her *Gravity and Grace:* "Suffering: superiority of man over God. The Incarnation was necessary so that this superiority should not be scandalous."[43] Let me conclude these particular remarks by suggesting that the belief that God somehow suffers with us is already more than half the answer to the problem of pain, for it proves that suffering is sometimes necessary, sometimes good—not in itself, of course, but in its consequences, above all in its involvements with love.

The climax of the theological problem of pain is the dogma of hell. This doctrine cannot be emptied of its core meaning, but its harshness needs to be tempered by a consideration of all relevant Christian truths according to the analogy of faith. Here I shall certainly not attempt this. I shall, in fact, limit myself to one quotation, namely from Julian of Norwich reporting in her *Revelations of Divine Love* what Christ in a vision said to her one day: "I may make all thing well, I can make all thing well, I will make all thing well; and thou shalt see thyself that all manner of thing shall be well."[44] Then, when Julian had a difficulty about hell, Christ responded: "That which is impossible to thee is not impossible to me. I shall save my word in all things and I shall make all things well."[45]

One cannot rightly oppose the private revelation of a mystic—*a fortiori* an uncanonized mystic!—to any genuine dogma. Yet such a revelation may very well be in accord with the *sensus fidelium* and so witness to a "feeling" that ought to be taken seriously. It may be that the "feeling" and the dogma are by no means really opposed, and the "feeling" may help us rightly to interpret the dogma. There are, no doubt, several ways in which the doctrine of hell can be represented so as not to oppose the doctrine of God's goodness and all-mercifulness. But in any case we can surely expect the ultimate explanation to be such that the most sensitive, most loving of mortals when he understands it will accept it, will approve it, will in joy exclaim: "All manner of thing will be well!" The most sensitive, most loving of mortals is not (supreme understatement!) so sensitive, so loving as God.

Conclusion

Louis Dupré has spoken of the Medusa face of evil.[46] This face according to the old Greek myth froze to stone anyone so audacious as to gaze upon it. It seems to me that evil has another face. The poet Coventry Patmore has a very wise as well as beautiful poem on pain, in which he calls pain "love's mystery." This leads me to conclude that the true face of evil is evil as God sees it, and evil as God sees it is, in this life, the test of love, the challenge of love, the very food of love. Indeed, must we not say that love's mystery is best understood when we contemplate the Son of God on the cross as he lays down his life for his friends?

Now at the end of the end I feel impelled to say with Job: "I have spoken as fools speak, of things far beyond my ken."[47]

Notes

1. Yves M. J. Congar, "The Problem of Evil," in Jacques de Bivort de La Saudee, ed., *God, Man and the Universe* (London, 1954), p. 410. For an account of the Berlin Academy essay contest see Paul Hazard, *European Thought in the Eighteenth Century* (London, 1954), p. 316.

2. Hume probably got the argument of Epicurus directly or indirectly

THE OTHER FACE OF EVIL   25

from Lactantius: *De Ira Dei ad Donatum,* XIII (PL, Vol. 7, col. 121), where it is cited. The Baron d'Holbach, who also gives this argument, mentions its source in Lactantius.

3. Andrew Marvell, "On Mr. Milton's Paradise Lost," lines 15–16. See in Dennis Davidson, ed., *Andrew Marvell: Selected Poetry and Prose* (London, 1952), pp. 159–161. Quotation from pp. 159–160. These lines from Marvell were called to my attention by Dr. John Klause in a book he is publishing on the poet. My debt to him, however, goes far beyond this. For some years we have carried on a lively controversy on the problem of evil in connection with a chapter in his MS. dealing with Marvell's views on this topic. I have found all our discussions and letters stimulating and helpful in the preparation of this paper. The two verses from MacLeish cited earlier occur on p. 11 of *J. B.: A Play in Verse* (Boston, last c. 1958).

4. *Aquinas* (Harmondsworth, Middlesex, 1955), p. 144.

5. *Confessions,* Book VII, Ch. 5.

6. Anthony Flew, *God and Philosophy* (New York, 1969), p. 48.

7. See Yves M. J. Congar, *op. cit.,* pp. 399 and 409.

8. See *Divina Commedia,* "Paradiso," Canto V, 11.19–22. G. K. Chesterton translates these verses as follows: "The mightiest gift that God of his largesse/Made in creation, perfect even as He,/Most of His substance, and to Him most dear,/He gave to the Will and it was liberty." *The Common Man* (London, 1950), p. 237.

9. Book III, Ch. IX, Paragr. 26 (PL, Vol. 32, col. 1284).

10. *Attack Upon "Christendom,"* cited from Robert Bretall, ed., *Kierkegaard Anthology* (Princeton, 1947), p. 459.

11. *Secular Humanism and Christianity.* Symposium at Alma College, Los Gatos, California, 1966 (privately printed), p. 102.

12. See C. S. Lewis, *The Problem of Pain* (New York, 1944), pp. 89–90.

13. For a present-day assessment of the view that blames all evil on sin, see Christian Duquoc, "New Approaches to Original Sin." *Cross Currents,* 28 (1978), 189–200, where on pp. 197–198 we read: " 'Why do evil, suffering and death exist in a creation that is good?' On this point, the theologian does not possess any secret, for Scripture does not deliver any. On the contrary, Scripture accentuates the question, since it makes the finished character of the human being a consequence of creation. Man is a mortal being, he is dust. Death in Genesis 3 is not a punishment, but puts an end to a life of suffering and pain. What is involved in the doctrine, therefore, is no longer an answer to the problem of evil, but the idea that history is in our hands, since the evils that we produce are our evils. As for other sufferings, those that derive from nature or from chance, we can combat them, and perhaps reduce them, but we cannot abolish them since they belong to our created existence. . . .

"The major discontinuity with the Augustinian theory of sin is that modern theologians no longer seek in sin an explanation for evil. . . . The conditions of finite existence escape all religious explanation. The sages, Job or the author of Ecclesiastes have taught them modesty." Duquoc's article appeared originally in *Lumière et Vie,* XXVI (Jan.–Mars, 1977).

14. *Utilitarianism,* Library of Liberal Arts (Indianapolis, c. 1957), pp. 305–306.

15. See Viktor E. Frankl. *Man's Search for Meaning: An Introduction to Logotherapy* (Boston, c. 1959), p. 115. For the quotation from Nietzsche see p. 106.

16. Cited from Piet Smulders, *The Design of Teilhard de Chardin. An Essay in Theological Reflection* (Westminster, Md., 1967), p. 288.

17. See, for example, the review of J. Z. Young, *Doubt and Certainty in Science* by M. A. MacConaill in *Month,* 6 (1951), 382–383.

18. Cited from "No Requiem for Theothanasia," *Herder Correspondence,* 4 (1967), 149. Cf. the statement of Gabriel Marcel: "For it is all too clear—and I have probably not pointed this out explicitly enough—that in spite of all the arguments that theologians and philosophers have had recourse to since the beginning, it is in the existence of evil and innocent suffering that atheism finds its permanent revitalizing bases." In "Contemporary Atheism and the Religious Mind," *Philosophy Today,* 4 (1960), 261.

19. *Much Ado about Nothing,* Act V, sc. 1, lines 35–36. It is Leonato speaking.

20. Ninian Smart, "Omnipotence, Evil and Superman," in Nelson Pike, ed., *God and Evil: Readings on the Theological Problem of Evil* (Englewood Cliffs, N.J., c. 1964), pp. 105–106.

21. *The Discovery of God* (New York, 1960), p. 176.

22. "The Mystery of Evil," in Elizabeth Pakenham, ed., *Catholic Approaches* (London, 1955), p. 26.

23. *Op. cit.,* p. 24.

24. *The World and the Individual* (New York, c. 1959), II, p. 340.

25. *The Other Dimension: A Search for the Meaning of Religious Attitudes* (New York, 1972), p. 399.

26. Friedrich von Hügel, *Essays and Addresses on the Philosophy of Religion,* First Series (London, first publ. 1921, repr. 1949), pp. 218–219.

27. A. E. Taylor, *Does God Exist?* (London, 1948), pp. 9–10.

28. Jean Daniélou, *The Lord of History* (London, 1958), p. 101. The quotation from Mohandas K. Gandhi is taken from his *An Autobiography: The Story of My Experiments with Truth* (Boston, 1968). I have cited it from Jeffrey G. Sobosan, "Experiments in Truth: Gandhi's Spirituality," *Spiritual Life,* 18 (1972), 198–213. See p. 205. The phrase "the vale of soul-making" is taken from a letter of Keats to his brother and sister written in April of 1819. See M. B. Forman, ed., *The Letters of John Keats,* 4th ed. (London, 1952), pp. 334–335.

29. Cf. G. K. Chesterton, *Saint Thomas Aquinas* (New York, 1933), pp. 131–132.

30. A. E. Taylor, *op. cit.,* p. 74. Note that even Hume's Philo would agree with Taylor in principle. Hume has him say: "Let us allow that, if the goodness of the Deity (I mean a goodness like the human) could be estab-

lished on any tolerable reasons a priori, these (evil) phenomena, however untoward, would not be sufficient to subvert that principle, but might easily, in some unknown manner, be reconcilable to it." Part XI of *Dialogues concerning Natural Religion,* ed. by Norman Kemp Smith. Library of Liberal Arts (Indianapolis, c. 1947), p. 211. Cf. Nelson Pike, "Hume on Evil," in Nelson Pike, ed., *op. cit.,* p. 97.

31. Abraham Maslow, *The Farther Reaches of Human Nature* (New York, c. 1971). The context gives us: "Transcendence of death, pain, sickness, evil, etc., when one is at a level high enough to be reconciled with the necessity of death, pain, etc. From a godlike, or Olympian point of view, all these are necessary, and can be understood as necessary. If this attitude is achieved, as for instance it can be in the B[eing] -cognition, then bitterness, rebelliousness, anger, resentment may all disappear or at least be much lessened" (pp. 271–272).

It may be helpful to give here a few brief quotes from saints and mystics on this matter: Let us begin with St. Margaret Mary Alacoque, who comes right to the point: "Without suffering one cannot love," she tells us. See André Jean Marie Hamon: *Vie de Ste Marguerite Marie* (Paris, 1924), p. 445. Similarly, St. Ignatius Loyola tells us that "The flame of divine love never rises higher than when fed with the wood of the cross," and, again, "Suffering endured for the love of Jesus Christ should be reckoned among God's greatest benefits" (Maxims of St. Ignatius, from a privately published work). St. Teresa of Avila goes so far as to say: "To die, Lord, or to suffer! I ask nothing else of Thee for myself but this." *Life. The Complete Works of St. Theresa of Jesus,* ed. by E. Allison Pears (New York, 1946), Vol. I, p. 297. The same saint in her typically picturesque style tells us: "Perfect souls are in no way repelled by trials, but rather desire them and pray for them and love them. They are like soldiers: the more wars there are, the better they are pleased, because they hope to emerge from them with the greater riches." *Way of Perfection. The Complete Works,* Vol. II, p. 163. St. Thérèse of Lisieux, St. Teresa's spiritual daughter, warns us against illusion: "Let us not fancy we can love without suffering, without suffering deeply." *Collected Letters of St. Thérèse,* ed. by A. Combes, transl. by Frank J. Sheed (New York, 1949), p. 101. I conclude these illustrative statements with a few lines from Julian of Norwich's *Revelations of Divine Love:* "When we come up and receive the sweet reward which grace hath wrought us, then we shall thank and bless our Lord, endlessly joying that ever we suffered woe. And that shall be for a property of blessed love that we shall know in God which we might never have known without woe going before." Edited from the mss. by Dom Roger Hudleston (London, 1927). p. 87.

32. (New York, 1966), p. 128.

33. Rom. 8:18.

34. The passage from Claudel is cited from Léon Joseph Cardinal Suenens, *Christian Life Day by Day* (Westminster, Md., 1964), p. 64.

35. *Joy* (New York, 1968), p. 48.

36. *Suffering* (New York, 1967), p. 125.

37. *Letters and Papers from Prison,* 3rd rev. ed. (New York, 1967), p. 198.

38. Jon Sobrino, *Christology at the Crossroads: A Latin American Approach* (Maryknoll, N.Y., c. 1978), p. 197.

39. *Ibid.* The quotation from Jürgen Moltmann is from *Der gekreuzigte Gott* (Munich, 1973), p. 217. Cf. the English translation, *The Crucified God* (New York, c. 1974), p. 230. Moltmann in this work cites a large number of theologians with somewhat similar views. See, for example, under "Index of Names" his references to Karl Rahner and Hans Urs von Balthasar.

40. See *Theological Studies,* 38 (1977), 569–571. Citation is on p. 570.

41. Cited in Robert McAfee Brown: "The Pseudonyms of God," in Herbert O. Schedler, ed., *Philosophy of Religion: Contemporary Perspectives* (New York, c. 1974), pp. 118–119.

42. Fyodor Dostoevsky, *The Brothers Karamazov,* Part II, Book V, Ch. 4 (New York: Grosset and Dunlap, n.d.), p. 267.

43. Simone Weil, *Gravity and Grace* (New York, 1978), p. 72.

44. *Op. cit.,* p. 53.

45. *Op. cit.,* p. 57.

46. See Louis Dupré, *op. cit.,* p. 391.

47. Job 42:3.

Ethos and Ethics
in the New Testament

Leander E. Keck

I

Traditionally, New Testament ethics has been concerned with the ethical or moral teaching contained in the NT. I want to comment on two aspects of this—namely, the content and the organization of the material. What constitutes the content, the material for NT ethics? If one understands ethics as critical reflection on behavior and its warrants, then one does not need to be a very sophisticated ethicist to see that there is very little ethics in the NT, and that what little reflection there is appears to be rather unconcerned with systematic thinking. Indeed, the word "ethics" does not even appear. True, Paul's letters normally have one or more sections devoted to exhortations for a certain range of behavior; yet these exhortations are grounded in a variety of warrants ranging all the way from what is appropriate to the Christ-event (e.g., Phil. 2) to Paul's own sense of what is proper (e.g., women's veils; 1 Cor. 11:2–17). How all this coheres is not easy to see. Moreover, the exhortations themselves, the moral teachings, constitute a plethora of counsels, commands and prohibitions that not only defy systematization but often turn out to be expressions of something deeper. Consequently, if one studies only the explicit moral exhortations, one misses a good deal of what NT ethics is all about. That is, if one assumes that ethics concerns not only the question, What is to be done? but also the question, Who is the doer and what are his or her communities?, then it is difficult to exclude anything in the NT from an analysis of its ethics. Failure to see this accounts, in part, for the fact that Jack Sanders was able to conclude that we ought to forget the whole thing.[1]

The material has been organized in two ways. One focuses on topics like sex, property, civil obedience, and then ascertains—usually in historical sequence—what major figures such as Jesus, Paul, John have to say about them. The other focuses on the figures in order to grasp the contours of each person's thought. Schnackenburg's *The Moral Teaching of the New Testament* is an example of the latter approach, and the recent sketch by Houlden, *Ethics and the New Testament,* combines both.[2] Both have the advantage of ordering the material in a way that is convenient to find; and neither blends everything because both distinguish the ethics of Paul from that of John, for instance.

But it is the disadvantages that interest me. I shall mention only one. The traditional approach tends to obscure the early Christians. When attention is riveted to the ethical teaching, however it may be organized, the focus is on the responses but the stimuli are in the shadows; the study of NT ethics becomes an analysis of answers to questions that are merely mentioned in passing, as if they were hooks on which to hang ideas. When the people are ignored, we begin treating NT ethics as the application of principles, ideals, or theology. This would actually be the ethics behind the NT or the ethics based on it, but not the ethics of it or in it, for the NT does not ignore its readers in order to think abstractly. The NT literature was not addressed "to whom it may concern," nor is it an anthology of religious texts published and sold in the bookstalls of antiquity—a kind of "the best of the best sellers." It is a compilation of texts addressed to Christian communities facing particular problems. It was the readers and their problems that evoked the writing of this literature. In a word, we do not understand the ethics of the NT until we get hold of the ethos of the early Christians.

To what extent is concern for the ethos really new? Clearly, the original readers of the NT have been studied many times. Indeed, modern historical criticism is based on the recognition that every text has a context in light of which it is to be read. In fact, beginning students are frequently overwhelmed by the amount of cultural and religious history that they are expected to learn before they get to the NT itself: mystery religions, emperor worship, Gnosticism, Stoicism, Hellenized Judaism, Essenes, Zealots, Pharisees, Sadducees, Dead Sea Scrolls, papyri, Nag Hammadi texts, Josephus, etc., etc. Still, the ethos of the early Christians has not yet been reconstructed.

By ethos I mean what is customary, habitual. Ethos includes a customary way of thinking and acting, a pattern of values, a style.

We have learned a great deal that is necessary to know if we are to reconstruct the ethos, things like language level, socio-economic status, the place of slaves and the character of anti-Semitism. But we still do not have in focus the ethos of the early Christians.

Of the many reasons for this that might be mentioned, I shall deal briefly with only one. The ethos of the people has not come into view until now because we have been imprisoned by our own categories, namely, we have spoken about Hellenistic influences on Christianity. This way of talking implies that there was an entity called "Christianity" that was subject to various influences from the outside. It is the legacy of the old contamination theory of Church history. But such a view implies that Christianity exists apart from Christians. To come right to the point by oversimplifying, one should speak less of Hellenistic (or Jewish) influences on Christianity and more of Christianity's influence on Hellenism and Judaism as embodied in the ethos of particular communities. To speak of Hellenistic influences implies that Hellenism is the intruder. Actually, it was precisely the opposite. It was Christianity, that is Christian preachers and their message, who intruded into the ethos of people and communities. It was Christianity that disturbed the ethos of synagogues, households, trade guilds and the like, at least in the first generation. In the early decades, it was the Gospel that was the foreign element, the factor introduced from the outside that influenced an ethos already in existence. I suspect that one reason we have not seen that sufficiently is that we have been trapped by our own ethos of talking about Hellenistic influences on Christianity, and that has blurred our historical and sociological perspective. But changes are under way, moving rapidly.

It may be useful to mention some things that have happened in the past decade.[3] Beginning in 1972 there emerged within the AAR/SBL a working group called the Social World of Early Christianity. Participants include archeologists, students of NT, patristics and social theory. The group focused on Antioch as a test case. A comparable group has been formed to study ancient Israel. There is a growing stream of publications, such as Gager's *Kingdom and Community*,[4] and the recent book by a prolific young German scholar, Gerd Theissen, *A Sociology of Early Palestinian Christianity*.[5] I only hope that this interest in the sociology of early Christianity is not merely another fad. The task is too important to appear and disappear like a meteor.

The task has numerous levels or components, and therefore calls for a participation from a spectrum of scholars. First, it is nec-

essary to know a great deal more about the ethos of these people before they were Christianized. A surprising amount of information
has already been gathered about things like family structure, education, guilds, population shifts and land use, slavery, legal procedures and the like. Grant's recent book, *Early Christianity and
Society,* contains this kind of information, as does Malherbe's *Social
Aspects of Early Christianity.*[6] Fortunately, there is a growing corps
of classicists also concerned with such matters. Students of early
Christianity, including patristics, will be conversing more with
these colleagues than they have in the past, just as advocates of a
literary approach to the Bible have been conversing with literary
critics recently. Second, we need to read the early Christian literature with different questions and sensibilities. In addition to looking for clues that help us reconstruct the history of doctrine, we
shall be looking for signs of the early Christian ethos, sometimes explicit, often detectable only to the eye trained to see. Moreover, we
need to use and test various sociological theories and models, recognizing that model is a heuristic device, not a straight jacket, and
that logically incommensurate models can nonetheless be used in a
complementary way because they illumine different facets of the
evidence. Third, developing an interest in an ethological approach
to the New Testament does not mean abandoning other approaches
but complementing and correcting them. For example, it comple-
ments form and redaction criticism by correlating literary strata
with communities more precisely; it corrects the prevailing approach to the history of theology that is based on a simple evolutionary development of ideas, and so produces the history of the
theology that should have been if professors had issued guidelines
for it.

II

Even though our interest is in the ethos of communities, contrasting Jesus and Paul is a useful way into our topic. Comparing
where they worked and what they talked about in their respective
contexts should give us a clue to the importance of ethos for an understanding of their ethics.

To begin with, Paul's mission was restricted to cities, whereas
Jesus worked in the villages and the countryside. Even if he visited
Jerusalem more often than the Synoptics report, he was never at
home there; his language is rooted in the villages and countryside
of Galilee. Moreover, so far as we can tell, Jesus' disciples also came

from Galilean villages, whereas Paul's associates came from the cities in which he worked.

This fundamental difference prompts us to ask whether there are traces in Jesus' teaching of the villager's world, especially its antipathy toward the city; conversely, we want to know whether Paul reflects an urban view of the world. Paul traveled extensively on land, but he never mentions the countryside or villages; he draws his major metaphors from urban, commercial life.[7] This suggests that the countryside was scarcely present in his consciousness. By contrast, Jesus' metaphors of the Kingdom were drawn from rural and village life. He also expresses contempt for a man wearing finery, for such persons live in "king's houses" (Mt. 11:8), normally located in cities.[8] Given a fundamental antipathy in antiquity between the country and the city, it is interesting that neither Paul nor Jesus mentions this explicitly; each simply moves within his own orbit.

A second difference appears with regard to economic security. The Jesus tradition urges people not to be anxious for the morrow. Although Jesus did not require self-impoverishment apart from exceptional cases like the rich young man, he did regard wealth as a danger and an obstacle to entering the Kingdom. Only rarely did he associate with persons of means, like Zacchaeus,[9] and never did he urge anyone to work. He himself had left his shop and had called fishermen to forsake their nets in order to wander about the countryside, accepting food from those who shared it with him and his troupe of mendicants.

Paul too traveled around with an entourage, and accepted the hospitality of persons like Lydia (Acts 16:11–15) and Titus Justus (Acts 18:5–11), whose relation to Paul was that of a patron to a client. The Australian classicist E. A. Judge has analyzed this relationship in light of prevailing patterns in antiquity.[10] Whereas Jesus accepted hospitality from his hearers as he moved about, Paul made the household of his patron the base of operations and accepted support money from the Philippians *after* he had left that city. Paul was proud of the fact that he continued to work with his hands (1 Cor. 9:3–18) and refused to accept money from his hearers even when in need (2 Cor. 11:7–11).[11] Above all, Paul urged the Thessalonians to "admonish the idle" (1 Thess. 5:14) and exhorted everyone to work with his hands as he had previously admonished them. He was concerned for the reputation of the Christian group and for the financial independence of everyone in it (1 Thess. 4:11–12). This difference between Jesus and Paul makes sense when the ethos of both is placed in context: Jesus in the villages, Paul in the cities.

Theissen has emphasized the importance of city life as the unquestioned foundation of Hellenistic Christianity. He also regards the radical statements of the Jesus-tradition with regard to property as a reflection of the ethos of the wandering prophets who, like Jesus, forsook everything in order to go from village to village among the marginal folk of the countryside.[12] Theissen also distinguished those sayings of Jesus that were treasured by the wandering charismatics from those cherished by the settled Christian villagers, and so tried to account for the coexistence of two types of ethics in the Synoptics, indeed, a two-tiered ethic—one for the perfect who wandered, one for the less perfect who stayed home. Be that as it may, the fact is that although Matthew 10 mentions the need to give hospitality, its real focus is on the need to live by receiving it. Paul, on the other hand, never summons his Christian readers to join him in moving about but urges them rather to give hospitality to those who do (Rom. 12:18; 16:1–2).[13] These Christians do not appear to be wandering preachers so much as Christians pursuing business affairs.

Above all, Paul's letters contain not a word of warning about wealth[14]—a fact that is all the more striking in view of the growing consensus that Paul's converts were not as poor as romantics like to make them. Paul's associates and converts included those who had houses large enough to accommodate the house Church, had enough wealth to take each other to court (1 Cor. 6:1–8), travel about, own slaves, eat and drink so conspicuously as to embarrass those who had little to eat at the Church supper (1 Cor. 11:17–22).[15] The moral values of this stable artisan and merchant class in the Hellenistic cities were quite different from those of the villagers, the fisherfolk, and the farmers of Palestine. The ethics of Jesus and the ethics of Paul reflect this difference. The Jesus-tradition contains a summons to make a radical decision, in the spirit of "let the dead bury their dead," but Paul, somewhat like his Stoic counterparts, called for an inner distancing from the things of this transient world (as in 1 Cor. 7:29–31). He did not call for deliberate rootlessness.

Third, Jesus and Paul and the groups they crystallized had quite different attitudes with regard to Jews and Gentiles, even though both Jesus and Paul were Jews and proud of it. To be sure, in the Hellenistic cities the Jews were minorities whereas in Galilee they were probably the majority. Nonetheless, it is increasingly

clear that Palestine, and especially Galilee, was far more Hellenized and had a higher percentage of non-Jews than our prevailing
image warrants. The more the Hellenistic non-Jewish element in
Palestine comes into view, the more striking the fact that Jesus apparently had nothing to do with it. Whether Matthew 10:24 is authentic or not, the fact is that Jesus apparently *did* restrict his
mission to "the lost sheep in the house of Israel" (also v. 6). Nor
does Jesus show any concern to go to the Samaritans or to Hellenized Jews, though he had ample opportunity to do so. He seems to
have avoided the more Hellenized towns, like Caesarea, Tiberias,
Sepphoris, Caesarea-Philippi, Gaza, etc. Theissen rightly calls the
Jesus movement a renewal movement within Israel. Matthew's picture is sound at this point: the mission to the gentiles is not to be
traced to the mission of Jesus but to the mandate derived from the
resurrection.

Paul, on the other hand, believed himself called to be an apostle to the gentiles. The faith of gentiles came as no surprise to him,
nor are gentile believers exceptions to the rule. For Paul, gentiles
are on a par with Jews as far as salvation is concerned. Accordingly, what Jesus apparently never thought about—the admission of
gentiles to the people of God[16]—Paul insisted on. As a renewal
movement, the work of Jesus was restricted even to a rather limited range of Jews. Paul, on the other hand, created an entirely new
community, one which in principle included persons of all cultures,
races, clans, economic and social status.[17] Jesus' task was differentiating the eschatological people of God amid the empirical people,
but Paul's task was to integrate a newly constituted people of God.
Jesus set out to distinguish the prepared from the unprepared, the
repentant from the unrepentant, but Paul set out to integrate the
repentant Jew with the converted gentile into a single Church.

The difference between Jesus and Paul manifests itself in the
language of social control, namely, the Jesus tradition refers to gentiles negatively; Paul does not.[18] Being like a gentile is something to
be avoided. Jesus contrasted love of enemy with the mutual love
which gentiles, like tax collectors, manage to achieve (Mt. 5:47); he
urged people not to pray like gentiles (Mt. 6:7).

He called upon his followers not to lord it over others the way
gentile rulers do (Mk. 10:42; Lk. 22:25). The Lukan version of the
call not to be anxious over food and drink points out that the gentiles ("nations of the world") seek these things. The harshest thing
of all was said to a gentile woman who asked Jesus for help: "It is
not right to take children's bread and throw it to the dogs" (Mk.

7:27). If one doubts that Jesus really said such things and argues that the Church attributed them to him, one must remember that the Church which gave us the Gospels was itself more and more gentile so that it is hard to think that the Church coined all such words. One negative use of "gentile" is certainly not from Jesus himself, namely, Matthew 18:17 where the ultimate punishment for the recalcitrant Christian is exclusion from the community, "let him be to you as a gentile and a tax collector." However, one simply cannot get rid of this anti-gentile bias entirely from the authentic Jesus tradition. Paul, on the other hand, claims he even lived like a gentile if that would facilitate the Gospel (1 Cor. 9:20–21).

Fourth, as noted, Paul was creating a new community, but Jesus was trying to renew an old one. The boundaries of the Jewish community vis-à-vis the gentile world apparently posed no explicit problem for Jesus. But the boundaries are precisely at the heart of Paul's problem. Consequently, the question that Jesus and Jewish Christianity faced concerned the proper way to be a faithful Jew readied for the Kingdom; the question of whether practicing Judaism was important or not never crossed their minds. The Jesus tradition is therefore concerned with the proper way to observe Sabbath, whereas Paul shows not the slightest interest in this question. For Paul the problem was whether observing any special day was religiously significant (Rom. 14:5; Gal. 4:10). Conversely, Paul's problem was the proper meaning of circumcision, a question that probably never occurred to Jesus. Nor did Jesus, for his part, reflect on whether his disciples could attend gentile religious festivals, something that Paul had to address in 1 Corinthians 10. If one is justified in saying that Jesus radicalized the law's demand, then one certainly cannot say the same for Paul.

Because Jesus was sifting an eschatological community from an empirical community, those who heeded his word found themselves at odds with parents, brothers and sisters, as well as neighbors and synagogues. In the villages where everybody knew everybody else's business, the slightest deviance from the inherited ethos could be the occasion for debate and harassment. Consequently the Gospel tradition has a great deal more about persecution and intra-family wrangles than do the letters of Paul. Paul's mission sought not to divide families but to keep them together. Among gentiles Paul's mission did not divide communities so much as it sought to create them, although it did divide the Jewish communities. Still, this division does not figure prominently in Paul's ethics.

Jesus' message did not intrude into the ethos of his hearers in the same way as did Paul's Gospel. In Palestine, Jesus' message was a summons to the authentic core of the ethos already functioning. That is why he could call for repentance. In such a context, Jesus' ethic was one of clarification by differentiation. In Paul's case, matters were more complex. On the one hand, he summoned his Jewish hearers to confess that the Messiah is Jesus, and to be baptized into Christ along with gentiles who, he insisted, must be free to retain much of their gentile ethos. Because Paul also insisted that there is one Lord's table for all believers, Jew and gentile were to eat together because in Christ neither circumcision nor uncircumcision matters any more. Thereby the traditional meaning of circumcision, as a mark of the people of God among gentiles and of a sacred ethos, was dissolved. Paul never urged Jewish Christians to stop circumcising their sons and abandon Jewish customs, as he was accused of doing (Acts 21:21). Yet the accusation was not altogether unfair, because when Paul told the Corinthians that they should feel free to buy anything sold in the meat market (1 Cor. 10:25–26) he did dissolve the dietary laws for any Jewish member of the Church. On the other hand, when Paul summoned gentiles to faith, he did not ask them to clarify the meaning of their inherited ethos or to relocate its center, but to abandon polytheism, obeisance to astral beings, certain practices and their participation in religious cults (1 Thess. 1:9–10; Gal. 4:8–10; 1 Cor. 6:9–11; 1 Cor. 10). In their place, they were to adopt elements of an ethos deeply influenced by Judaism and its scripture. In short, the ethic of Jesus called for a return to a given, but the ethic of Paul undertook to fuse elements of two givens into a new one. No wonder the Corinthians regarded him as too conservative and the Jerusalem Christians as too radical.

It would be rewarding to explore further the contrasts between Jesus and Paul, but we have seen enough for our purposes. Jesus was trying to purify an ethos,[19] Paul was trying to shape a new one. This is why many of the ethical matters with which Jesus dealt were of no concern to Paul, and why some of Paul's problems were beyond the horizon of Jesus. Once this is seen, we can no longer discuss the ethics of Jesus and the ethics of Paul abstractly, as if each was a matter of applied theology only. The ethics of both was rooted in the ethos of the communities in which they worked.

Gauging the success of Paul is difficult. The Apocalypse of John shows no real trace of Pauline influence in Asia Minor. In one matter, Paul was flatly repudiated—namely, freedom to eat meat that had been offered to idols. Although Christians followed Paul in dis-

solving the differences between clean and unclean food, they rejected his teaching that one was free to eat anything sold in the meat
market, that is, idol meat. The Seer on Patmos indicts the Church
at Thyatira for tolerating a prophetess who teaches Christians to
eat food offered to idols (Rev. 2:20). The same practice was advocated at Pergamum (Rev. 2:14). Repeatedly, later writers repudiate
this freedom to eat such food, silently bypassing the fact that Paul
had taught the opposite.[20]

III

Gradually there emerged a characteristic Christian ethos. One
way of getting a sense of how the Christian ethos was developing is
to look at the literature from the closing years of the first century—
Luke, Matthew, John, 1 Clement, Revelation, and perhaps Ephesians, Hebrews, James and Didache as well. We shall not look at all
of it here, of course. We shall focus on one question: What happened
to the ethic of Jesus, so deeply rooted in the ethos of Palestinian villages, when this tradition was taken over by urban Christians in
Antioch? In some ways it is remarkable that the Jesus tradition, addressed to the ethos of Palestinian village life before the Revolt,
should have been written down in Gospels produced in city
churches after the war. Probably many of the stories and sayings of
Jesus disappeared, perhaps because they dealt with things no longer germane. Be that as it may, our concern is with what was preserved and used even though it was rooted elsewhere, and in some
ways was in tension with the ethos of those who wrote Gospels.

We shall look at the Gospel of Matthew, probably written
around A.D. 90 in Antioch, a major urban center with a strong Jewish community. Relationships with this community dominate the
horizon of this Gospel. After the fall of Jerusalem, the rabbis who
reconstructed Judaism at Jamnia sought to consolidate Jewish life
on the basis of a modified Pharisaism, which became rabbinism. Including in the liturgy a curse on the heretics made it impossible for
Jewish Christians to continue any significant participation in Jewish worship. This action, taken in Matthew's time, cast its shadow
over the Antiochene Church.

The Christian community in Antioch had a long and distinguished history, going back half a century to the days when Hellenistic Jewish Christian refugees brought the gospel to the city,
shared it with gentiles as well as Jews, and forged an "interracial"
Church until this was broken up by emissaries from James. Antioch

may also have been the place where John was written, as well as the Odes of Solomon, the oldest collection of Christian hymns. Shortly after Matthew's time, we hear of early gnostics in Antioch: Saturnilos, Cerdon (later associated with Marcion), and Basilides for a time. Its most famous bishop, Ignatius, became a martyr. In Matthew's day, Christians in Antioch did not compose a single unified community with branches in local house churches; rather, the Christian movement was rather diverse and was soon to be splintered into factions. Indeed, we shall see that Matthew himself had to contend with intense internal friction among his readers, though he does not appear to have contended with gnostics.

Matthew attempts to deal with internal and external problems at the same time. He does this by uniting disparate elements of the Jesus tradition in such a way as to provide simultaneously an internal criterion for the community and a legitimation against external critics in the synagogue. I shall deal briefly only with the internal problems, recognizing that I am sharing an agenda to be pursued more than results achieved.

At this point it is useful to interject a word about the disparate traditions mentioned a moment ago. I assume that Matthew used Mark, the sayings tradition called Q, and material unique to Matthew, labeled M. Whether Q was a document or several collections of sayings, partly written and partly unwritten, is not clear. It is also possible that Q, like M, is not uniform because it incorporates stages of tradition. More important, the materials in Matthew point in different directions. For example, Matthew 10:5-6 has Jesus forbid a mission to anyone but Jews, but 28:16-20 has him command a world-wide effort among gentiles. Jesus commands love for the persecutor and forgiveness without limit, and also bitterly pronounces doom on his critics, the Pharisees. Even within the Sermon on the Mount there are tensions. The disciples are told so to live that their good works can be seen, and also that their alms, prayer and fasting be not seen. One might account for these divergencies by regarding them as reflecting either different stages of the same tradition or different groups, or both. In any case, Matthew is an eclectic Gospel. As we shall see, the social significance of the literary integration of these traditions is community consolidation, and the compositional technique is a symptom of a particular mode of consolidation. Form indeed follows function.

The internal difficulties in Matthew's Church are so numerous and so diverse that one scarcely knows how to sort it all out. Let me mention some of the problems. Many converts drift away either because of duress or because the demands are too high. Others remain but do not really belong; they are like weeds in the wheat. The purists want to expel them. Others need disciplinary action, and those doing the disciplining need proper procedures. Some leaders put on airs, wanting to be called "rabbi." When harassment comes, some betray their brothers and hatred arises. The love and devotion of some have grown cold. Antinomians argue with rigorists. Eschatological hope has waned among some, has been overheated among others. Prophets appear who mislead the people.[21] It is far from clear how these problems fall into patterns that can be associated with particular groups or stages. Nonetheless, as a working hypothesis, I want to concentrate on the problems produced by the charismatic prophets.

Gerd Theissen has emphasized the view that early Palestinian Christianity was deeply influenced by wandering charismatics, prophets filled with the Spirit who preached a radical gospel. He believes that these wandering charismatics "shaped the earliest traditions and provide the social background for a good deal of the synoptic tradition, especially the tradition of the words of Jesus." It is this group that has transmitted the radical ethic of Jesus, especially its call for surrender of home, family, possessions, and self-protection. For Theissen, these prophets embodied this radical teaching; that is, "the ethical radicalism of the synoptic tradition is connected with this pattern of wandering, which could only be practised and handed down with any degree of credibility by those who had been released from everyday ties of the world, who had left hearth and home, wife and children, who had let the dead bury their dead, and who took the lilies and the birds as their model. It only had a chance in a movement of outsiders." Consequently, he concludes, the radical ethics of the Synoptics had scarcely any place in urban, secure Christianity.[22]

Although Theissen has often rolled things together that need to be distinguished more precisely, he nonetheless suggested a solution to a long-standing problem—where to locate Q. Virtually every study of Q is faced with the question: Where can we locate a community whose understanding of the Gospel is restricted to the sayings of Jesus, and which appears to have no soteriological interest in the passion and resurrection? What I am proposing is that Q is not to be associated with a settled community primarily but precisely with the wandering charismatic prophets. Theissen himself observed in passing that the radical sayings tradition was in part handed on by groups that circulated Q, but to my knowledge he has not developed the idea fully.[23]

The recent study of Q by Edwards has tabulated the features of what he calls the Q community: (a) keen expectation of the imminent return of Jesus as the Son of Man; (b) urgency to prepare for his coming by fulfilling the demands placed upon people by the coming judge; (c) the preaching of these demands by appropriating the preaching of Jesus himself; (d) the conviction that Jesus now inspires prophets to speak in his name; (e) awareness that those who live by the demands will experience rejection and persecution.[24] Moreover, Suggs has argued that Q regarded Jesus as divine Wisdom's last emissary, whose rejection caps the history of rejecting prophets and persecuting the righteous.[25] I believe Suggs's view comports with that of Edwards.[26] Together, what they describe as the community of Q fits very nicely with Theissen's portrait of the wandering charismatics. In other words, instead of looking for a *place* where Q was at home, perhaps we should look to a *group* that was not at home but characteristically on the road. In these circles Jesus' death and resurrection did not precipitate a reconsideration of the meaning of the Jesus-event as atonement for sin, but was regarded as vindication of his message and a legitimation of theirs. These prophets took up where the work of Jesus, and of John the Baptist, had been broken off.

Like Jesus, the charismatic prophets, whose message is represented in Q, oriented their preaching to the ethos of the countryside and its villages where they appealed especially to the poor. Because they associated wealth with corruption and infidelity to God, the wandering prophets excoriated the wealthy and congratulated the poor. Concern for private ownership was disdained, as was the ethos of the wealthy. They themselves were forbidden to take even the most essential provisions for travel.[27] What matters is treasure with God. Second, the demands of radical discipleship were not understood as a flat repudiation of the Jewish ethos but as a clarification of it, as a reconstituted center of what was always there, or should have been. Third, response to their message disrupted the existing social fabric and its warrants, for it challenged elements of the prevailing ethos at sensitive points[28] and divided families. Fourth, rejection was turned into confirmation. Being rejected only underscored the conviction that they were right. Only a few will enter the narrow door; the rest will be destroyed. The harassed stand in the lineage of the persecuted prophets. But they need not fear, for God cares for each one; besides, the opponents can do no more than kill the body. Finally, the nearness of the judgment requires everyone to be ready and to avoid compromising one's resolve.[29]

These prophets with their radical demands and stringent criteria for the Christian community came to Antioch. We do not know when they arrived or how influential they were. Perhaps prophetic influences that were found in Antioch from the start[30] were strengthened when the Q people arrived after the fall of Jerusalem. This possibility would help explain the intensified animosity between Church and synogogue. That is, tensions between Jewish Christians and the synagogue turned to bitterness because of pressure from Jamnia on the one hand, and because of the radical ethos of the charismatic preachers on the other. The arrival of the radical charismatics would only have confirmed the Jamnian view that the Jewish community must be rid of this influence.

Somewhat less speculative is the likelihood that the presence of the charismatic prophets created problems for the Antiochene Church. Several considerations point in this direction. (a) The Q tradition contains the warnings against those who call Jesus Lord but do not do as he commanded (Mt. 7:21; Lk. 4:46). This is a sign that the prophets were not afraid to indict other Christians.[31] I suspect that in Matthew's parable they are the servants who volunteer to get the weeds out of the wheat (Mt. 13:24–30). Because the prophets speak in the name of the Lord, they may well have become intolerant, eager to purify the community living by a less rigorous, urban ethos. (b) Käsemann has proposed that the Sentences of Holy Law, formulae of divine retribution on judgment day, were developed among early Christian prophets. Such formulations are now scattered remnants of an early, common phenomenon in Palestinian Christianity.[32] One such saying is found in Q, namely, the saying that whoever acknowledges Jesus before persons, Jesus will acknowledge before God, and whoever denies Jesus will be denied by Jesus (Mt. 10:12–15, par.).[33] It is likely, therefore, that the Q material was developed at least in part by charismatic prophets.[34] In other words, the more Antiochene Christianity developed within the structures of a stable, relatively secure urban ethos, the more of a disturbing factor were the charismatic prophets.

The Gospel of Matthew shows how the Evangelist handled these problems. I shall merely identify several things that Matthew did. First, when he incorporated the Q material into a Markan structure he subordinated it to a passion Gospel and thereby defined the proper context for the radical sayings. Sociologically, this implied that the prophets were not to be the arbiters of the rest of the community but the reverse.

Second, he deprived the prophets of their right to serve as vigilantes within the community. He did so by including the parable of the weeds in the field and of the fish in the net, both of which insist that the Church is impure until the end. He did so by insisting that the Church is not to be imaged solely as an itinerant, homeless, structureless movement but as a house built on a rock named Peter.[35] It is Peter who has the keys of the Kingdom, not the prophets. Matthew also prescribed proper procedures to be followed in matters of Church discipline, and he put those procedures in a context that emphasized forgiveness of the brother (Mt. 18).[36]

Third, Matthew muted the emphasis on the Holy Spirit that was the basis of charismatic authority. On the one hand, although he retained the saying about blasphemy against the Spirit (perhaps because it was in both Q and Mark), he ended his Gospel without a word of the promised Spirit. This contrasts sharply with Luke and John; what these two Gospels insist on—presence of the Spirit— Matthew bypasses completely. It is not accidental that Matthew has only those exorcism stories which he got from Mark, and that he omitted the story of the strange exorcist whom Jesus accepted even though he was not part of the group (Mk. 9:38).[37] Moreover, the way Matthew ended the Gospel implies that Jesus is present with the Church precisely in the tradition that Matthew has just written down.

Fourth, Matthew retained Q's warnings about wealth and the security it offers, but at the same time he transformed the Beatitudes.[38] He did not spiritualize them by turning "Blessed are you poor" into "Blessed are the poor in spirit," but he made sure that those who were not economically poor—that is, the Antiochenes[39]—could be included in the blessing. Likewise, the hunger and thirst that is satisfied is no longer limited to real hunger but becomes a yearning for righteousness. In other words, Matthew guarded against a literal socio-economic interpretation of the Beatitudes, and so adapted them for his urban, more "middle-class" Church.

Fifth, Matthew asks that the community distinguish prophet from prophet, because there are false prophets around (Mt. 24:11). Q has the saying about good fruit from good trees, and about fruitless trees being cut down and burned (Mt. 7:16–20; Lk. 6:43–44). In the mouths of the prophets, these sayings were directed against the Church. But Matthew introduced the saying by urging, "Beware of false prophets who come to you in sheep's clothing," and so directed the warning against the prophets themselves. He did not repudiate prophets categorically, of course. Then he rewrote another Q tradition into a scarcely veiled warning to the prophets—on judgment day some of you who prophesied, cast out demons and did mighty works in Jesus' name will nonetheless be repudiated because you did not do God's will (Mt. 7:21–23)—namely the will of God marked out by the whole Gospel of Matthew and the ethos to which it points. Above all, Matthew retained the Markan warning that the Church must watch out for prophets who claim to be Christ himself speaking, for these lead many people astray (24:5,11).

In short, Matthew dealt with the charismatic prophets by affirming their rigorous message as a criterion for the Church, by setting limits on their freewheeling activity, and by emphasizing the institutional aspect of the Church. It is not surprising that Matthew's Gospel contains so many tensions that its ethics appears to be contradictory. Matthew's own ethics cannot be ascertained by simply compiling the exhortations of Jesus, nor by adding up the warrants for the many values, nor by appealing to a dominant motif like discipleship. Matthew's ethics can be got at only by seeing how the radical ethic of Q was being handled by a Christian deeply committed to both radical discipleship and institutional life. In other words, to study Matthew's ethics we need to see his hermeneutic of ethical materials that moved from one ethos into another.

IV

What, then, has this limited excursion into the theme of ethos and ethics in the NT shown us? First, that the social realities of early Christian communities must be treated far more seriously, as more than the "setting" within which ideas and values were taught.

Second, that the diversity of the NT is part of an even greater diversity within early Christianity, and that this diversity cannot be accounted for solely on the basis of a proliferation of theological trends. Nor can the diverse theological trends be regarded as the effects of social factors only. Rather, one should be alert to the continuing interaction between them. Changed circumstances modify theology and ethics, and modified theology and ethics introduce new factors in the circumstances. One would very much like to know, for instance, what new problems were generated for the Antiochene ethos by the writing of Matthew.

Third, if this sort of foray into Matthew should be extended to the rest of the NT, the consequence for the authority of NT ethics today would be significant. Let me simply identify three areas where this might appear. (a) We would need to consider the authoritativeness not only of the explicit ethical teachings but also of the early Christian precedent for dealing with certain types of situations. The strategies devised, and the kinds of moral reasoning involved, may turn out to be as important as the verbalized results. Discovering that would entail discerning the degree to which NT precedents are paradigmatic for our own situations. This process is already under way, of course, but attending to ethos and ethics in the NT might contribute to it. For instance, if Paul is free to modify Jesus' teaching on divorce, and if Matthew is free to modify Jesus' teaching on wealth, to what extent are we free to modify Paul's teaching about homosexuality and Matthew's attempt to constrain the prophets? In other words, using the NT in Christian ethics could no longer be a matter of applying the text as if it were canon law; it would be a matter of learning how to appropriate and extend canonized precedent.

(b) What are we to do with Q and what it represented? If it is true that Matthew domesticated the radical message of the charismatic prophetic tradition because of the dangers he saw in it for his own situation, are there situations today in which Matthew's undertaking should be reversed? Given the eclectic nature of Matthew's Gospel, it is not surprising that some Christians will be drawn to one strand (like Q), others to another (like Matthew himself). How do we assess the tacit hermeneutic operative in this diverse attraction? That is a major question for not only ethics and ethos in the NT but for Christian ethics and ethos across the board. A major contribution of the study of ethos and ethics in the NT is the placement of this question on our agendas. The authority of the NT manifests itself to the degree to which it can make this question unavoidable.

(c) The more tightly the NT ethic is bound to the particularities that it addressed, the less authoritative are the particular commands and prohibitions. Specific teachings about things like idol meat, Sabbath observance, sexuality, property, work, taxes, are so shaped by the social realities of particular times and places that only by careful analogical reasoning can one derive guidelines for today.

In the long run, then, the significance of NT ethics may lie not so much in what it says should be done as in what it says about the doer and his or her community of faith. In this way, the NT may well be as great a disturber of our own ethos and ethics as it was originally. Should that happen, we would discover what its real authority is.

Notes

1. Jack T. Sanders, *Ethics in the New Testament* (Philadelphia: Fortress, 1975); see my review in *ATR* 60 (1978) 98–100.

2. Rudolf Schnackenburg, *The Moral Teaching of the New Testament*, trans. by J. Holland-Smith & J. O'Hara. (Freiburg: Herder; London: Burns & Oates, 1965; 2d German ed. 1962). J. L. Houlden, *Ethics and the New Testament* (Harmondsworth, England: Penguin Books, Ltd., 1973; American ed., New York: Oxford University Press, 1977).

3. Earlier attempts to deal with the ethos were sketched in my article, "On the Ethos of the Early Christians," *JAAR* 42 (1974) 435–40.

4. John G. Gager, *Kingdom and Community. The Social World of Early Christianity* (Englewood Cliffs: Prentice Hall, 1975).

5. Gerd Theissen, *A Sociology of Early Palestinian Christianity*, trans. by John Bowden. (Philadelphia: Fortress, 1978).

6. R. M. Grant, *Early Christianity and Society* (New York: Harper and Row, 1977; Abraham J. Malherbe, *Social Aspects of Early Christianity* (Baton Rouge: Louisiana State University Press, 1977).

7. Agricultural metaphors are not wholly absent from Paul, of course (cf. e.g., 1 Cor. 3:5–9; 9:7–10; 15:35–44; 2 Cor. 9:6; Gal. 6:7–9). They take their place alongside metaphors drawn from military life (1 Cor. 9:7a; 14:8; 2 Cor. 10:3–6; Phil. 2:25) or athletics (1 Cor. 9:24–27; Gal. 2:2; Phil. 3:14) in that they generally deal with matters of behavior. Paul's soteriological metaphors, on the other hand, are associated with social relationships especially as they are institutionalized in the city: emancipation, adoption, acquittal.

8. For a discussion of Jesus' attitude toward cities, see Theissen, *Sociology*, 47–59.

9. G. W. Buchanan goes too far in claiming that not only were Jesus' audiences "predominantly wealthy" but that he associated primarily with the upper classes. "Jesus and the Upper class," *NovTest* 7 (1974) 195–209, esp. 202–209.

10. E. A. Judge, "Paul and Classical Society," *Jahrbuch für Antike u. Christentum* 15 (1972) 19–36.

11. Theissen has suggested that Paul had to defend his custom because there arrived wandering nonworking preachers who appealed to Jesus' words. See "Legitimation und Lebensunterhalt: Ein Beitrag zur Soziologie Urchristlicher Missionäre," *NTS* 21 (1975) 192–221.

12. See "Wanderradikalismus. Literatursoziologische Aspekte der Überlieferung von Worte Jesu im Urchristentum," *ZThK* 70 (1973) 245–71. An English translation of this article, basic for Theissen's work, is available: "Itinerant Radicalism: The Tradition of Jesus' Sayings from the Perspective of the Sociology of Literature," *Radical Religion* II 2, 3 (1975) 84–93.

13. Paul's exhortation to hospitality is not found in the letters to Cor-

inth, Galatia and Philippi; this may reflect Paul's own problems with wandering preachers in those places (see note 11). Nowhere does Paul urge Christians to cease welcoming wandering preachers. Hospitality was part of the emerging Christian ethos.

14. See Nils A. Dahl, "Paul and Possessions," in *Studies in Paul* (Minneapolis: Augsburg, 1977), 22–39. Dahl observes that Paul mentions money matters frequently, but seems to avoid the actual terminology for it. Paul's warnings against greed stand in lists of vices.

15. Theissen has emphasized this socio-economic factor in Corinth. See "Soziale Integration und sakramentales Handeln. Eine Analyse von I Kor. XI 17–34," *NovTest* 16 (1974) 179–206.

16. At most, the universality of Jesus' message and mission is implicit. Hahn does not note this sufficiently. Ferdinand Hahn, *Mission in the New Testament* (Naperville: Allenson, 1965), Chap. 2.

17. Nils A. Dahl has seen the social implications of Paul's doctrine of justification by faith. See "The Doctrine of Justification: Its Social Function and Implications," in *Studies in Paul*, 95–120.

18. "Gentile sinners" (Gal. 2:15) may not have been typical of Paul, for the context suggests that Paul is expressing precisely the Jewish attitude toward gentiles, which he opposes. Romans 1:18–32, though interpreting the gentiles, does not actually specify this; nor does 1 Corinthians 6:9–10 identify these "unrighteous" with gentiles. Nor do 1 Corinthians 5:1; 10:20; 12:2; 1 Thessalonians 4:5 uses "gentile" as an expression for a life-style to be avoided, even though a critical attitude is implied. What is absent from the genuine Pauline letters is found in Ephesians 4:17—"You must no longer live as the Gentiles do. . . ."

19. Robin Scroggs argued that Jesus and his movement fit all the criteria for a sect, yet he must admit that Jesus did not attempt to found a "closed organization which would further rigidify the boundaries between the establishment and the outcasts." Nor does Scroggs discuss evidence which suggests that Christianized Jews remained participants in synagogue life until after the Revolt. "The Earliest Christian Communities as Sectarian Movement," in *Christainity, Judaism and other Greco-Roman Cults. Studies for Morton Smith at Sixty*. J. Neusner, ed. 4 vols. (Leiden: Brill, 1975) II 1–23.

20. The whole phenomenon of Paul's attitude toward dietary matters, to be distinguished from his counsel about them, has been studied by John C. Brunt, *Paul's Attitude Toward and Treatment of Problems Involving Dietary Practice: A Case Study in Pauline Ethics*. Ph.D. Diss., Emory University, 1978; see espec. Chap. 7.

21. The dissertation by William J. Thompson, S.J., provides a good discussion of these problems. *Matthew's Advice to a Divided Community* (Rome: Biblical Institute Press, 1970). See also his recent study, "A Historical Perspective in the Gospel of Matthew," *JBL* 93 (1974) 243–62.

22. *Sociology*, 10, 17, 115 resp.

23. "Wanderradikalismus," 255, 267 n. 64.

24. Richard A. Edwards, *A Theology of Q* (Philadelphia: Fortress, 1976), 63, 148–9.

25. M. Jack Suggs, *Wisdom, Christology and Law in Matthew's Gospel* (Cambridge: Harvard University Press, 1970), Chaps. 1–3.

26. Unfortunately, Edwards does not come to grips with Suggs's contention, but dismisses it without even representing Suggs adequately (*op. cit.*, 59). Nor does Edwards come to grips with Siegfried Schulz's study, but is content to say that the effort to distinguish layers of tradition is "not only questionable but unnecessary" (*op. cit.*, 147 n. 2). See Siegfried Schulz, *Q. Die Spruchquelle der Evangelisten* (Zurich: Theologischer Verlag, 1972).

27. Paul Hoffmann emphasized the importance of the prohibition against purse, bag, sandals and staff (Lk. 10:4; Mt. 10:9–10): the wanderer thereby manifested poverty, defenselessness, and a "pacifistic" demeanor. *Studien zur Theologie der Logienquelle* (Münster: Aschendorff, 1972), 312–26.

28. Hoffmann, *op. cit.*, 309–11, calls attention to the contrast between the "peace" which the Q missioners were to bring (Lk. 10:5–6; Mt. 10:12) and the increasingly Zealotic mentality of the times.

29. Hoffmann, *op. cit.*, 13–79, insists that the Q group maintained the expectation of the imminent coming of the Son of Man, and did not modify its hope in light of disappointment over the delay of the Parousia, as Dieter Lührmann argued in *Die Redaktion der Logienquelle* (Neukirchen: Neukirchener Verlag, 1969), 86.

30. Acts reports that prophets, including one Agabus, arrived from Palestine (Acts 11:27–28); according to 13:1–3, there were also resident prophets in Antioch.

31. I am not persuaded by D. Hill's attempt to separate the false prophets of Matthew 7:15 from the charismatics in 7:21–23, and to identify the former as the Pharisees of Matthew's time. "False Prophets and Charismatics: Structure and Interpretation in Matthew 7:15–23," *Biblica* 57 (1976) 327–48, espec. 340–48.

32. Ernst Käsemann, "Sentences of Holy Law in the New Testament," in *New Testament Questions of Today*, trans. by W. J. Montague (Philadelphia: Fortress, 1969), 66–81, espec. 79. Klaus Berger has criticized Käsemann's essay. "Zu den sogennanten Sätzen Heiligen Rechts," *NTS* 17 (1970) 10–40.

33. Matthew 10:15 and Luke 10:12 contain the expression, "I say to you." Schulz regards this as a formula of charismatic preaching that goes back to the oldest level of Q. Therefore, he concludes, this supports Käsemann's view of Sentences of Holy Law. *Op. cit.*, 60.

34. Berger, *op. cit.*, has denied precisely this link because he found no explicit basis on which to associate the "Sentences of Holy Law" (he also denies they are "holy law") with charismatics. But what sort of explicit connection could be expected?

35. Eduard Schweizer has recently argued that for Matthew, Peter

and the Twelve are the necessary links between Matthew's own Church and Jesus, and that this link concerns first of all the teaching office. This insight comports better with my hypothesis than with Schweizer's own view that Matthew's church is a group of wandering charismatics. *Matthäus und seine Gemeinde*, SBS 71 (Stuttgart: Katholisches Bibelwerk, 1974), 155.

36. I doubt whether Thompson has identified the real reason why Matthew included the advice on how to reconcile a brother, namely, "because wickedness has become so widespread that most men's love has grown cold (24:12)." "An Historical Perspective," 262. Rather, the context shows that the discipline is to be exercised with restraint, probably because there is a tendency to uproot the wayward without due process or mercy.

37. Interestingly, Matthew does indeed have Jesus commission his followers to cast out demons, heal and raise the dead (10:1,8), but this occurs in the mission charge in Chapter 10, which is part of Jesus' own mission that is limited to Israel. This mission is superseded by the mission to gentiles after the resurrection, in Matthew's own time. And in the commissioning that ends the Gospel not a word is said about prophetic, charismatic, exorcistic work but only about making disciples by teaching and baptizing. Jack Dean Kingsbury, "The Verb AKOLOUTHEIN ("To Follow") as an Index of Matthew's View of his Community," *JBL* 97 (1978) 69.

38. Whether Luke added the woes (Lk. 6:24–26) or Matthew omitted them is difficult to decide; I suspect the latter is the case.

39. J. D. Kingsbury has recently assembled data suggesting the relatively affluent character of the Matthean Church. *Op. cit.* 67–8.

The Foundations of Paul's Ethics

Al Hiebert

Contemporary discussions of ethics tend to be bedevilled by two facts, contends Oxford Professor of New Testament, D. E. H. Whiteley.[1] First, we live in an age of "residual Christianity" when many who do not go to church still acknowledge certain moral standards that depend on Christian roots. Second, contemporary discussions of ethics tend to assume the possibility and validity of moral systems independent of God.

> To St. Paul this would have been unthinkable. God had made His will known to all men, who therefore stood under judgment. For St. Paul the sinner was not merely guilty of an offense against an impersonal code; he was in a state of deliberate rebellion against a personal God.[2]

For Paul, ethics was not merely a trivial part of theology as it has too often been regarded recently. It was rather "an essential and inseparable part of his entire corpus of thought, and its status is not diminished but enhanced by its integration with his 'dogmatic' theology."[3] This is because Paul as a true biblical Jew took the perspective of the Old Testament that based its moral precepts firmly on the nature of God and his saving acts, rather than attempting to develop self-contained and self-justifying systems of ethics as did the Greeks.[4]

In fact many of Paul's most significant theological expositions "are occasioned by the need to drive home some ethical point."[5] His letters so characteristically have an exposition of doctrine followed by moral admonition that he clearly regards morality as "dependent upon and inseparable from religious faith."[6]

This perspective stands in stark contrast to the sentiments expressed recently by William J. Byron, S.J., editor of the *Topics in*

Moral Argument series, when he endorsed the suggestion that "the most important religious question around today is whether Christianity has anything to add to secular humanism."[7] Byron's reply to that question is "that Christianity's addition to secular humanism comes in the form of replies to the boundary questions of life—birth, death, suffering, failure, meaninglessness."[8] Granted, Christianity in general and Pauline ethics in particular make major "additions" to secular humanism in its replies to these boundary questions of life. But in the perspective of the present writer, Christian ethics, even when limited for purposes of the present discussion to the writings of Paul, provides answers that are fundamentally superior to any provided by any form of secular humanism, not only in its treatment of the "boundary questions" of life but also in its treatment of the basic foundational questions of life such as what ought to be our life's goal, pattern, motives and dynamic power. The present discussion seeks to explore Paul's teaching on these foundational ethical concerns in hopes that this framework may be helpful in our attempts to understand the proper meaning of various detailed biblical ethical injunctions, and in our attempts at proper biblical casuistic application of Christian ethics to the various specific circumstances of life.

Drane points out that part of the problem in contemporary academic works in ethics may be due to their virtually exclusive preoccupation with judging particular actions like murder or abortion.[9] Such particular casuistic judgments can be made only on the basis of assumed answers to the foundational questions that are the concern of this paper. Clearly the moral philosopher or theologian who attempts such casuistic judgments without first answering the foundational questions on which they depend is proceeding with a culpable reckless abandon that may well cause both him and his hearers to stray grievously.

It is also worth noting that so much discussion of Christian ethics tends to fail to gain wide acceptance beyond a particular Christian subculture because of its tendency to begin at the point of the particular casuistic applications of biblical teaching to specific situations. If instead we were to begin with a transcultural analysis of the foundations of Christian ethics, our discussions might well win a hearing beyond the particular Christian subculture from which we may happen to speak.

Perhaps the most obvious contrast between the approach taken by Paul and that taken by secular humanists (and many of their "semi-Christian" admirers) is that Paul's approach is clearly theonomous and the approach of the humanist is typically autonomous. This strong contrast emerges clearly in each of the fundamental issues discussed below. To Paul, God has defined the proper goal, pattern, motives and dynamic of man's life just as much as he has defined the behavior patterns of the subhuman universe studied by the physical scientist. Man is no more free to set the laws of morality for himself autonomously than he is free to set the laws of physics, chemistry or biology for himself autonomously.

Paul also assumes that man is a moral being, possessing not only the capacity for moral judgment but betraying also a certain content of moral law "written in the heart" (Rom. 2:14, 15). Paul recognizes that man is morally free rather than being a moral robot and so regards man as responsible for his own moral and spiritual behavior (Rom. 6–7). Still, he also recognizes man's propensity to sin, to ignore God's requirements and transgress God's will (Rom. 3:10–13, 23). This means a spiritual conversion is essential before a person could even consider living a proper Christian ethic according to the goal, pattern, motive, and dynamic of life as defined by God (Rom. 5:1; 6:23; 12:2; II Cor. 5:17). Without such a supernatural transformation from being a rebellious sinful character to being a "new creature in Christ" it is impossible to consider a Christian ethic life-style as described by Paul. In short, only one who has truly become a Christian can realistically expect to live according to the foundations of Christian ethics that Paul describes.

A. The Goal of the Christian Life

Paul describes the goal of a believer's daily growth and experience in various complementary ways. In the first chapter of his letter to the Ephesians Paul writes that God has "predestinated us . . . to the praise of the glory of his grace" (v. 5, 6) and "predestinated us . . . that we should be to the praise of his glory" (v. 11, 12). In II Corinthians 3:18 he writes: "But we all, with unveiled face beholding as in a mirror the glory of the Lord, are being transformed into the same image from glory to glory, just as from the Lord, the Spirit."[10] In I Corinthians 10:31 he states this foundational principle in very practical terms: "Whether, then, you eat or drink or whatever you do, do all to the glory of God."

The Westminster Shorter Catechism of 1647 summed up this principle to say the goal of the Christian life is "to glorify God." If glorifying God means to reflect to others the glorious moral character of our God, then Paul adds details concerning what that entails:

"He chose us in Him before the foundation of the world, that we should be holy and blameless before Him" (Eph. 1:4); "speaking the truth in love, we are to grow up in all aspects into Him, who is the head, even Christ" (Eph. 4:15). Repeatedly Paul exhorts us to reflect in our lives God's moral character of infinite holiness, love and truth as Christ did, against whose stature we are to measure our growth and progress toward our goal (Eph. 4:13; 5:8f; Col. 1:28, 29; I Thess. 5:5ff). We are to be "conformed to the image of His Son" (Rom. 8:29) who in turn is the express image of God (II Cor. 4:4; Col. 1:15). In short, the goal of our moral development and action is to be morally perfect as a reflection of our God's character in us.

B. The Pattern of the Christian Life

If our goal is to glorify God by becoming like Christ then the pattern by which we are to progress toward that goal is already implied to some extent. If in glorifying God we are to reflect his moral nature in our lives, then all revelations of God's moral nature become sources of guidance for our moral development and action. In the first two chapters of his letter to the Roman Christians, Paul alludes to God's general revelation, particularly in creation (1:18–21, 27) and conscience (2:14, 15), as a revelation of God's will regarding the pattern of man's life, though he gives more attention to how sinful men reject and pervert God's general revelation than to the potential moral instruction to be gained by this mode of revelation. Though he warns that a conscience may be a weak revelation of God's intended life pattern (I Cor. 8:7, 10, 12; 10:25), yet it is to be obeyed (Rom. 14:14, 20, 23; I Cor. 3:10; Ti. 1:15). Whitely argues, however, that in all fourteen Pauline occurrences of the word conscience (suneidesis), it is used only in the negative sense of remorse for a wrong already done.[11] In this usage a "good conscience" indicates only a "freedom from remorse" rather than a positive selective power enabling us to know what is right before we do it such as the "practical wisdom" (phronesis) of Aristotle.

Another mode of God's revelation to us is his special revelation in scripture including the writings of Paul. Thus, he does not hesitate to command or order his readers authoritatively (II Thess. 3:4, 6, 12; I Cor. 7:10), though at times he pleads with them on the basis of grace given him (e.g., Rom. 12:3; 15:15) and appeals to their judgment of the truth of his instruction (I Cor. 10:15).

For Paul the most vivid revelation of God's pattern of life for us is the example of Christ (I Cor. 11:1; Rom. 15:3, 7; II Cor. 8:9; Phil.

2:5ff; Col. 3:13; Eph. 5:2) as the supreme "visual aid" of God's nature and will. God's example also is used as a determining factor for our life's pattern (Eph. 4:32; 5:1; Col. 3:10). Paul even refers to himself as an illustration of one who follows Christ's pattern and suggests we can in turn follow him (I Cor. 4:16; 11:1; Phil. 3:17; I Thess. 1:6; 2:10; II Thess. 3:7), though he would have been horrified at any suggestion that his example carried any weight at all as a second authority independent of Christ (Gal. 2:20).

The believer is not merely to imitate Christ externally, but rather the believer's life "in Christ" is to be continuous with Christ's life, so as to bear the imprint of his example to the extent of identification with Christ in his death to sin by crucifixion and resurrection in a new life of allegiance to our new Lord showing our family resemblance to our heavenly family (Gal. 2:20; 3:27; Rom. 6:1–18; Col. 2:12; 3:1–3). Tinsley has given us an informative examination of Paul's references to the imitation of Christ and has shown how they are paralleled in the Gospels.[12]

The believer's position "in Christ" is for Paul the only basis for an authentic Christian ethic that is guided both by the "law of Christ" (I Cor. 9:21; Gal. 6:2) and by the "mind of Christ" (I Cor. 2:16). Longenecker suggests that Paul means the "law of Christ" to include both the teachings of Jesus as the true interpretation of God's will for man (Rom. 12–14; I Cor. 7:10–11; Acts 21:35; I Tim. 5:18) and Jesus' tangible portrayal and paradigm of God's standard as suggested by his expression "according to Christ" (Rom. 15:5; Col. 2:8) and his frequent appeals to Jesus' character (Rom. 15:3, 7, 8; I Cor. 11:1; Eph. 5:2, 25ff; Phil. 2:5–11; I Thess. 1:6).[13]

This new law of the Messiah abrogates the Mosaic covenant for the believer in Christ (Rom. 7:1–6; Gal. 3:23–26; Eph. 2:15). Yet at the same time, it explicates more fully the divine standard in continuity with that code; so it is for Paul the external expression of God's eternal principles, setting the bounds for the believer's life and indicating the quality and direction which his action should take within those bounds.[14]

This "law of Christ" becomes a realistic pattern of life only by the energizing dynamic of life described by Paul as the "mind of Christ," by which he seems to indicate the activity of the indwelling Holy Spirit that enables the believer "in Christ" to discern God's will and make the proper ethical judgment (casuistic application) in each given situation (Rom. 12:2; Phil. 1:10; I Thess. 5:19–22).

Thus on the question of who or what ought to determine the pattern of life for the believer Paul agrees with Jewish teaching that right and wrong are "not defined by the reason and conscience of men, naive or reflective, nor by national custom or the *consensus gentium*, but by the revealed will of God."[15]

Likewise, Paul thought of the ethical life primarily in terms of righteousness and its expression, not just in terms of civic rightness or social propriety. Ancient codes of jurisprudence, while represented as having been given by a god or gods, stressed almost exclusively the idea of civic and social rightness; and modern man usually thinks along the lines of what is proper on the horizontal plane alone. But Paul, in accord with the Hebraic tradition upon which he built, thought first of righteousness and then of rightness, believing that only in the first is there an adequate basis for the second.[16]

Paul has properly been described as the apostle of liberty both in his stress on the Christian's release from the bondage of striving to obey the Mosaic law perfectly and in his emphasis on the Christian's liberty concerning so-called *adiaphora*. Yet he recognizes certain prudential considerations that turn even *adiaphora* situations of Christian liberty into moral ones. In these grey areas he raises a number of considerations that should aid the concerned believer to determine a proper pattern in areas of Christian liberty.

For example, even though one's conscience may be faulty ("weak") so as to give itself scruples about things that are actually in the legitimate realm of Christian liberty (I Cor. 8:7, 10, 12; 10:25), yet he warns us not to violate our conscience and thus, to our own minds at least, rebel against God (Rom. 14:14, 20–23; Ti. 1:15). He warns also that not all legitimate behaviors are edifying (I Cor. 10:23) and some may even enslave us unduly (I Cor. 6:12). Also we must consider how our exercise of liberty may affect others (Rom. 14; I Cor. 8), how it affects our bodies as God's temple (I Cor. 3:16, 17), and how it affects our thinking (Phil. 4:8). In short, Paul urges us to do everything we do "heartily as unto the Lord" (Col. 3:23) and "to the glory of God" (I Cor. 10:31), while abstaining even from "the appearance of evil" (I Thess. 5:22).

Some of Paul's injunctions, however, clearly have local temporal application to unique historical situations such as the "present distress" in Corinth in the light of which he recommends celibacy (I Cor. 7:26), though he recognizes that many do not have that gift

(I Cor. 7:1–9). His instructions concerning women's head-covering (I Cor. 11:3–16) may also fall more properly in the category of prudential considerations with moral overtones only in the light of the local cultural symbolic meaning of women's head-coverings versus bareheadedness. Similar prudential decisions need to be made concerning matters of Jewish ceremonial and dietary laws that now are matters of Christian liberty in the unified Jew-Gentile body of Christ (Rom. 14; I Cor. 8).

Paul does not hesitate to spell out some very specific details concerning the patterns of social relationships incumbent on husbands and wives, parents and children, masters and slaves, citizens and rulers (e.g. Rom. 13:1–7; Eph. 5:21–6:9; Col. 3:19–4:1; Titus 3:1). Nor does he hesitate to name specific behaviors that the believer in Christ is to "put off" or "put to death" as characteristic of the old preconversion life and family resemblance (e.g. Rom. 1:21–32; Gal. 5:19–21; Eph. 2:23; 4:17–31; 5:3–7, 11, 12; Col. 3:5–9; I Tim. 6:3–11; Titus 3:2, 3). He is equally candid in his descriptions of the behavior patterns and virtues that God legitimately expects to characterize the "new creature" in Christ (e.g. Rom. 12–14; II Cor. 8; Gal. 5:22–6:6; Eph. 4:1–16; 5:15–6:20; Phil. 4:4–9; Col. 3:12–4:6; I Tim. 6:11, 12, 17–19; Titus 2:11–15).

But an indication of the proper view of life's goal and pattern can too easily be viewed as an arbitrary, voluntarist "divine command theory" of ethics without due consideration of Paul's teaching regarding both the proper motives by which the believer is to live as God wants him to live and the dynamic power by which the believer is enabled to live that kind of life.

C. The Motives of the Christian Life

1. Primary motive: agape love.

Paul makes it abundantly clear that we ought to be motivated to live a life of Christ-likeness reflecting God's glory motivated primarily by the kind of love for God and our fellow-men that God has so abundantly showed to us in rescuing us from the penalty and power of sin by Christ's sacrificial substitutionary death for us guilty rebels (Rom. 5:5–10; II Cor. 5:14–15). As Whiteley comments, this subject is "one of supreme importance, and must be treated either at great length or very briefly."[17] Time and space here do not allow the extensive treatment this subject warrants, but a few observations are essential.

In Galatians 5:13, 14 Paul seems to echo the teaching of Jesus (Matt. 22:36–40) that love is to be the primary motive of all our moral life in relation to God and man when he writes, "For you were called to freedom, brethren; only do not turn your freedom into an opportunity for the flesh, but through love serve one another. For the whole Law is fulfilled in one word, in the statement, 'You shall love your neighbor as yourself.' " This is not to suggest that love is to become the determining factor that distinguishes whether an action is morally right or wrong, good or bad as Fletcher and the situationists suggest.[18] For Paul, love is to be the strongest and best possible motivation for living as new creatures in Christ according to the patterns that God has revealed. Thus to understand love as a discriminating faculty in moral decision-making is to misunderstand its role in Paul's ethics. Love does not define the pattern by which we are to live; it defines the motive for living the most worthwhile life that we could live, namely a life "in Christ" reflecting God's glorious moral nature as expressed in all of his self-disclosures.

Paul's classic exposition of the nature of love in I Corinthians 13 describes love as being not only the fundamental motive that ought to underlie all our interpersonal relationships on the horizontal plane, but also as being the root of our faith and hope in our vertical relationships. In Galatians 5:6 he describes faith as "working through love." In his salutations to the Colossian and Thessalonian Christians he comments particularly on their faith, hope and love (Col. 1:4, 5; I Thess. 1:3, cf. I Thess. 3:6; 5:8).

Of the many metaphors that Paul uses to describe the relationship of the Church to her Lord, that of the most intimate loving relationship between bride and bridegroom (Eph. 5:21–33) best communicates the loving relationship that we are to experience with our risen Lord. This love for our bridegroom is most naturally expressed not only in our faith in his care and fidelity, not only in our expectant hope for his promised return, but also in joyful compliance with his slightest wish for us. This is why it seems as incongruous to call Paul's ethics a "divine command theory"[19] as it would be to call a young bride's devotion to her beloved a "bridegroom command theory" of marriage. The believer is best described as a bride in the ecstasy of newly wedded love delighting to please her beloved. Only if that bride degenerates into a cantankerous nag who resents her bridegroom's every loving wish as chore can Paul's ethics be viewed as a "divine command theory."

2. Auxiliary motives:

Still Paul is quite realistic in his assessment of our actual ethical motivation patterns. Though our moral action should always be prompted by our love for our Lord and for our fellows, we all do fall short of God's glory (Rom. 3:23), i.e., in this regard, love often is not the source of our ethical motivation as it ought to be. And so on occasion Paul relates his moral exhortations to such auxiliary motivations as the desire for reward, the fear of punishment, the obligations of various duties, and gratitude for the high and holy calling that believers have accepted in Christ.

a. *Desire for Rewards*—Moe points out that the idea of reward plays a smaller role in the Pauline letters than in the Gospels and that with good reason.[20] The word *misthos* (reward) is used only five times in Paul's letters (I Cor. 3:8, 14; 9:17, 18; Rom. 4:4) in only three passages. In Romans 4:2ff he rejects the notion that justification and salvation are gained as a reward for any kind of works. In I Corinthians 3 he contemplates the reward of faithfulness to one's calling and in I Corinthians 9 he speaks of the reward of an inner satisfaction he feels for being able to proclaim the Gospel without depending on support from his hearers.

b. *Fear of Punishment*—The fear of punishment is more prominent as an auxiliary motive voiced in Paul's preaching and letters. As in his missionary sermons he pointed to the impending day of judgment and divine wrath that threatens unrepentant sinners, so in his letters he warned of divine wrathful judgment that will surely come on those who continue in their sins (Rom. 2:5, 8; Eph. 5:5, 6; I Thess. 4:6; Gal. 5:21; I Cor. 6:9f; Col. 3:6).[21] This judgment Paul sees in inner organic relationship to sin (Gal. 6:7ff) so that in our temporal world already sin is punished by sin (Rom. 1:18–32). Though Christians need not suffer from a slavish fear of ultimate punishment, even they are admonished to fear an accounting before the judgment seat of Christ (II Cor. 5:10, 11) and to perfect their sanctification in the fear of the Lord (II Cor. 7:1; Eph. 5:21; Col. 3:22; Phil 2:12).

c. *Duty*—On occasion Paul indicates a duty, such as that children obey their parents in the Lord, simply because it is right (Eph. 6:1) or because it is the will of God (I Thess. 4:3; 5:18). He describes the duty of wives to be subject to their husbands as being "fitting in the Lord" (Col. 3:18).

d. *Gratitude*—But when he exhorts us to "walk in a manner worthy of the calling with which you have been called" (Eph. 4:1), to "walk worthy of the God who calls you into His own kingdom and glory" (I Thess. 2:12), to "walk in a manner worthy of the Lord, to please Him in all respects, bearing fruit in every good work . . . giving thanks to the Father, who has qualified us to share in the in-

heritance of the saints in light" (Col. 1:10, 12), to "conduct your-
selves in a manner worthy of the gospel of Christ" (Phil.
1:27), to
"be ambassadors for Christ with the ministry of reconciliation" (II
Cor. 5:19, 20) then the sense of duty wears rather thin and the sense
of deep gratitude and its attendant love gains strong ascendency.

> As this feeling of gratitude impels men to do the will of
> God and to please Him, the other motive—the thought of
> their calling—teaches them that this will is directed pre-
> cisely toward their own sanctification (I Thess. 4:3).[22]

The Christian ought to be as much motivated by gratitude for
Christ's sacrificial death as the bond-slave who voluntarily serves
the one who purchases his redemption from slavery (I Cor. 6:20;
7:23). Hence Christians ought not to regard their lives as their own
to direct as they please; they belong to the one who died for them
and rose again to be their loving Lord (I Cor. 6:19; Rom. 14:6–8,9; II
Cor. 5:14, 15).

D. The Dynamic Power of the Christian Life

Such a life lived to glorify God by a pattern expressive of God's
nature as revealed in his self-disclosures, motivated by love, is
clearly humanly impossible. It requires the supernatural indwelling power of the resurrected Christ in the form of the controlling
power of God the Holy Spirit. The lack of this absolute essential in
all non-Christian systems of ethics leaves them fundamentally impotent to transform sinners such as we all are. This consideration
shows up Byron's "most important religious question around today" to be such a mockery when he asks "whether Christianity has
anything to add to secular humanism."

Paul's ethics simply presupposes a regeneration and transformation of life effected by Christ through his Spirit. He taught neither salvation by moral renewal, nor the possibility of living the
Christian ethic apart from being "in Christ."

> It is because the believer is "in Christ," and therefore a
> "new creation," that life has become transformed (II Cor.
> 5:17); and it is because Christ is in the believer through the
> Spirit that Christians can be exhorted to live in obedience
> to the Spirit (Rom. 8:10–14). Apart from this foundation,
> the superstructure of the Pauline ethic has no rationale or
> support.[23]

In the discussion above concerning the pattern of life it was already noted that for Paul, the believer "in Christ" is guided both by the "law of Christ" (Christ's exemplary life and teachings) and by the "mind of Christ" (the indwelling Holy Spirit which enables the believer to discern God's will in each situation beyond those on which we already have God's will revealed). Although Paul's ethic is clearly theonomous rather than autonomous (i.e., its values are determined by the nature and will of God rather than by those of man as in speculative ethics), the moral discernment provided the believer by the "mind of Christ," the indwelling Spirit of God, does suggest a measure of moral autonomy. Moe takes this idea to its logical limit:

> It is ultimately the Spirit of God which not only gives men their moral impulses but also teaches them what is morally right. And therefore, *ideally* (italics added), Christians should not need any external guide nor even the moral teaching of the apostle, but each should know for himself what Christian morality is as well as what is Christian truth (Rom. 15:14f and I Cor. 10:15).[24]

This suggestion may, however, be somewhat too ideal to be realistically practical in view of the noetic corrupting effects of sin on the mind even of the believer "in Christ."

In Galatians 5:16–25 Paul describes the Christian life that is lived according to God's pattern of victory over the desires of our flesh (our evil propensities) as a "walk by the Spirit," a life "led by the Spirit," a life characterized by the "fruit of the Spirit," i.e., a life characterized as our Lord was by "love, joy, peace, patience, kindness, goodness, faithfulness, gentleness, self-control." In Ephesians 5:18 Paul exhorts us to be as controlled ("filled") by the Holy Spirit as the drunk is by wine. Only if we are thus controlled by God's Holy Spirit can we expect to live a life that comes anywhere near the goal, pattern and primary motive of life that Paul describes.

In short, Paul indicates that the indwelling Holy Spirit gives us the ability to know what is right and the power to do it. The believer is, however, still left with the responsibility to yield himself to the Spirit in both areas since the Spirit will not force Himself on anyone any more than wine will.

In conclusion, we may ask whether this Pauline foundational framework is primarily a deontological or a teleological ethics. On balance, though Paul is interested in the ultimate outcomes of our moral actions, such outcomes are not really the determining factors that make moral decisions and actions right or wrong, good or bad. He rather regards moral values as rooted in God's moral character revealed in his self-disclosures. Hence, Paul's ethics must be regarded as primarily deontological in nature.

As noted in the introduction, much discussion of Christian ethics fails to gain acceptance beyond a particular Christian subculture because of the tendency to focus on the particular casuistic application of biblical teaching to specific situations rather than focusing on foundational principles that could well have wider appeal. It is hoped that the present discussion of the foundational principles of Paul's ethics could serve as a basis for common commitment among Christians whose particular cultural ethos may well lead them to somewhat differing conclusions in certain areas of casuistry. In short, we may well differ in particular preferences of individual trees in the forest, but hopefully we can more readily agree on the overall shape of the Christian ethical forest in view of which we can better understand whether or not our favorite ethical trees properly fit into the "big picture" of the forest landscape.

In terms of Augustine's dictum: hopefully the above description of life's goal, pattern, motive and dynamic might introduce us to some Christian moral essentials on which we ought to have unity, even if we recognize that there are some nonessential casuistic applications on which we can tolerate liberty while maintaining "in all things charity."

Notes

1. D. E. H. Whiteley, *The Theology of St. Paul* (Philadelphia: Fortress Press, 1966), p. 209.
2. *Ibid.*
3. *Ibid.*, p. 205
4. C. H. Dodd, *Law and Gospel* (New York: Columbia University Press, 1951), pp. 10–11.
5. Whiteley, p. 205. Whiteley lists as illustrations of this the following "articles" of Paul's *kerygma* which are connected with moral exhortation: 1) The fulfillment of scripture (I Cor. 10:11); 2) The coming of the Messiah (Phil. 2:5–11); 3) The crucifixion (Rom. 14:15); 4) The burial (Rom. 6:4); 5) and 6) The resurrection and heavenly session (Col. 3:1, 2); 7) The sending of the Spirit (Gal. 5:25); and 8) The judgment (II Cor. 5:10).
6. Olaf Moe, *The Apostle Paul: His Message and Doctrine*, trans. by L. A. Vigness (Minneapolis: Augsburg Publishing House, 1954), p. 406.

7. William J. Byron, "Editor's Introduction," in James F. Drane, *Religion and Ethics* (New York: Paulist Press, 1976), p. 1.

8. *Ibid.*, p. 2

9. James F. Drane, *Religion and Ethics* (New York: Paulist Press, 1976), pp. 6–7.

10. Scripture quotations are taken from the *New American Standard Bible* (Philadelphia: A. J. Holman Company, 1973).

11. Whiteley, p. 210.

12. E. J. Tinsley, *The Imitation of God in Christ* (London: S.C.M. Press, 1960), pp. 134–165.

13. Richard N. Longenecker, "Pauline Ethics," *Baker's Dictionary of Christian Ethics,* ed. by C. F. H. Henry (Grand Rapids, Mich.: Baker Book House, 1972), p. 492.

14. *Ibid.*, pp. 492–493.

15. George Foot Moore, *Judaism* (2 vols.; Cambridge, Mass.: Harvard University Press, 1927), Vol. II, p. 79.

16. Longenecker, pp. 491–492

17. Whiteley, p. 232.

18. Joseph Fletcher, *Situation Ethics: The New Morality* (Philadelphia: The Westminster Press, 1966), *passim.* A full critique of Fletcher's view of the role of love in ethics would here take the discussion much too far afield. Many excellent critiques exist including for example, Norman L. Geisler, *The Christian Ethic of Love* (Grand Rapids, Mich.: Zondervan, 1973) and Erwin Lutzer, *The Morality Gap* (Chicago: Moody Press, 1972).

19. William K. Frankena, *Ethics* (2nd ed.; Englewood Cliffs, N.J.: Prentice-Hall, Inc., 1973), pp. 28–30.

20 Moe, p. 411.

21. *Ibid,*, p. 412.

22. *Ibid.*, p. 413.

23. Longenecker, p. 492.

24. Moe, p. 407.

The Zen of Ethics

Silvio E. Fittipaldi

It is not surprising that very little has been written about Zen ethics, nor is it startling that Zen is often characterized as amoral or antinomian. Even the most articulate of Zen writers who have been read in the West, D. T. Suzuki, seems to confirm that Zen is not interested in ethics. He wrote:

> Morality is regulative, art is creative. One is an imposition from without, the other an irrepressible expression from within. Zen finds its inevitable association with art but not with morality. Zen may remain unmoral but not without art.[1]

Suzuki thus identifies ethics with the "regulative." Zen, insofar as it is creative, he implies, is antiregulative or antinomian. However, Suzuki is not consistent in regard to Zen's antinomian character. In another place, he writes that antinomianism is "a pitfall for the follower of Zen against which constant vigil is needed."[2]

Immediately we seem to be confronted with a *koan:* Zen is antiregulative yet this antinomian characteristic is a pitfall.

Before confronting this *koan,* I want to make a few more introductory comments. Such remarks will inevitably throw light on the *koan* and make it more complex. First, from an historical perspective, Zen has been related intrinsically to Buddhism and affirms the Buddhist precepts. Zen also has been deeply influenced by Confucian principles. Thus, it would seem that Zen ethics is a creative synthesis of Buddhist and Confucian ethics. The point here is that there is an ethics in Zen in contrast to the implications of D. T. Suzuki.

Secondly, Suzuki does not absolutely deny that Zen is ethical though he comes very close to doing so when he defines ethics as "the application of logic to the facts of life."[3] Zen, it would seem, involves a "frame" of mind that cannot be circumscribed by any logic. Hence, if ethics is logic applied to life, then Zen has no one logic that can be applied and hence Zen does not have one ethics.

The first part of this article will face the question of Zen and Buddhism and logic and the dilemmas found in the interfacing of these themes.

The second part of this article will have a very different cast. In the above quote from Suzuki, in which he contrasts art and morality, he affirms that Zen is inevitably associated with art. I think that Suzuki gives us a clue here as to how one might approach Zen ethics. Suzuki does not consciously or unconsciously suggest what I will argue, but I believe my argument is in the spirit of his words. In *Zen Buddhism and Psychoanalysis* Suzuki describes an "artist of life." Such a person lives out of the source, the Buddha-Nature. All that goes to form this person—body, mind and personality—"is both the material on which and the instruments with which the person molds his creative genius into conduct, into behavior, into all forms of action, indeed into life itself."[4] In other words, Suzuki seems to suggest that ethics can be viewed not so much as a set of rules but rather as an art. Ethics is not denied but seen as the art of living.

It is the assumption of the second part of this article that Zen ethics is Zen art. Morality is not opposed to art but rather the behavior of a person is artful. To speak of Zen ethics is to speak of Zen art. The characteristics of Zen ethics would be the characteristics of Zen art or Zen aesthetics. The translation of Zen aesthetics to Zen ethics and the "ground" or "source" of those aesthetics will be the main point of the second part of this article. In the end, we will reach a Zen of ethics.[5]

1. *Zen, Buddhist Ethics and Logic*

In many of his writings, Suzuki discusses the relation between Zen and Buddhism. His view is not simply that Zen is derived from Buddhism nor that Zen has nothing to do, in essence, with Buddhism. The issue is much more complex. Historically, Zen is a development of the cross-fertilization of speculative Indian Buddhism with the concrete, practical, earthy spirit of the Chinese people.

Suzuki does not deny this. He explicitly affirms it when he points out that:

Undoubtedly the main ideas of Zen are
derived from Buddhism, and we cannot but
consider it a legitimate development of
the latter.[6]

Suzuki, however, is also aware of another approach to this question. He points out that the followers of Zen claim that they are transmitting the essence of Buddhism, that they have stripped Buddhism of all the doctrinal and historical paraphernalia and have penetrated to its core which is the spirit of the Buddha, a spirit that is not confined to Buddhism but is the spirit of life.[7] Shin'ichi Hisamatsu also suggests this when he writes:

Zen is not one particular school within
Buddhism; it is, rather, the root source
of Buddhism.[8]

Suzuki further affirms this when he argues that the articulation of the Zen experience or its intellectual content could be supplied by a system of thought which is not necessarily Buddhist.[9]

Thus, Zen can be perceived as independent of Buddhism yet as the "root source" of Buddhism. While Zen has its historical roots in Buddhism, it is not confined to Buddhism. In its manifestation of the spirit of the Buddha, Zen by that fact transcends Buddhism.

What has just been said in regard to Zen and Buddhism can be directly applied to Zen and Buddhist ethics and Confucian ethics. Zen, insofar as it is, historically, a manifestation of Buddhism and Confucianism, affirms the Buddhist and Confucian ethics and follows their precepts. At the same time, Zen is not bound absolutely into these ethics but is the "root source" of them.

Furthermore, Zen not only claims to be the root source of Buddhism and Buddhist ethics, but also of any religion and any ethics. Suzuki writes:

Zen, being life itself, contains everything that goes into the
make-up of life; Zen is poetry, Zen is philosophy, Zen is morality. Wherever there is life-activity, there is Zen. As long
as we cannot imagine life to be limited in any way, Zen is

present in every one of our experiences. . . .

When I say that Zen is life, I mean that Zen is not to be confined within conceptualization, that Zen is what makes conceptualization possible, and therefore that Zen is not to be identified with any particular brand of "ism."[10]

This quote leads us into the discussion of Zen and ethics as logic as applied to life. It also gives a glimpse of the meaning of the title of this article—"The Zen of Ethics," i.e., the Zen claim to be the root source of ethics.

In an illuminating passage in his *An Introduction to Zen,* Suzuki states that ethics "is the application of logic to the facts of life."[11] Suzuki criticizes such a practice. Logic involves words and concepts that may or may not correspond to the facts of life. Zen is concerned with the facts and not with their logical representation. The application of logic to life is topsy-turvy. We ought to operate the other way round. First, there is life. Then, there is logic as an expression of life. Sometimes that expression is adequate. Often it is not a satisfactory representation. "Zen wants to live from within. Not to be bound by rules, but to be creating one's own rules—this is the kind of life which Zen is trying to have us live."[12] This kind of life is not antinomian. Rather, it is art—"Life is an art," Suzuki proclaims.[13]

In Zen, ethics is neither Buddhist nor logical. Yet neither Buddhism nor logic is eschewed. Rather they are seen to be what they are, limited expressions of life. Zen has to do with life directly. Thus, Zen can be seen as the "root source" of ethics, for ethics fundamentally arises from life before it points back to life. The way a human person is in the life of which he or she is a part, is ethics. And in Zen that is art. It does not affirm or deny law. Zen is neither antinomian nor legalistic. It is, rather, the source of law.

Hence, we do not seek the ethics of Zen. We, rather, search out the Zen of ethics which is to seek ethics as art, the art of living.

II. *Ethics as the Art of Living*

It is the purpose of this section to develop the suggestion that Zen ethics is the *art* of living. It is the contention of this section that the characteristics of Zen art are the characteristics of a Zen ethic. Thus, "living" in a Zen manner can be depicted as the art of living. Shin'ichi Hisamatsu, in his challengingly beautiful book, *Zen and the Fine Arts,* describes seven interrelated characteristics of Zen art. These characteristics will be translated into an ethics. Another way to say this is: the characteristics of Zen aesthetics are applicable to Zen ethics. The seven characteristics are: Asymmetry, Simplicity, Austere Sublimity or Lofty Dryness, Naturalness, Subtle Profundity or Profound Subtlety, Freedom from Attachment, and Tranquility.[14]

1. Asymmetry

I would imagine that the eyes of many readers of this article have been trained or conditioned to appreciate regularity and balance and evenness in art and in life. We can marvel at the extraordinary symmetry of Salvador Dali's *Last Supper* with its focus on Jesus, the earthly and cosmic Christ. Many people are quite sensitive to color coordination and are literally pained when they experience a clash of colors. Interior decorating manifests the decorator's eye for balance and appropriateness. The monastic orders applied such criteria to life-style and the highest compliment that could be made to a person was that he lived a "regular" life.

In symmetrical art, the gracefulness of the forms evokes feelings of perfection and flawlessness. Everything is in its place. Everything has a place and resides in it. There is nothing out of place. Perfection has been achieved. Beauty has been created. This small part of the world is in order.

The human task is, then, to bring this order to all of life, to personal life and to social life. Perfection becomes the goal. To be perfect is to live a life of virtue when alone as well as with others. It is the accomplishment of fairness and balance and hence justice. To be perfect is to know one's place and to live gracefully in that place, to be consistent and regular so that one's life manifests the development of a beautifully (balanced, orderly) designed tapestry. In the end, the person will be characterized as holy.

Zen art, however, breaks with *these* ideals of perfection and grace and holiness. Symmetry is perceived as a form imposed on life. Zen art is, rather, an expression of life in its asymmetricalness as well as its symmetricalness, in its disorderliness as well as its orderliness, in its imbalance as well as its balance, in its unfairness as well as its fairness, in its injustice as well as its justice, in its irregularity as well as its regularity, in its flaws as well as its flawlessness, in its awkwardness as well as its gracefulness, in its imperfection as well as its perfection, in its unholiness as well as its holiness. Mu-chi's *Persimmons,* to choose a painting that might be known to the reader, are not all the same. Each has a somewhat different texture. Nor are they balanced in relation to each other. Rather they fall on the paper as six apples might find their place on your kitchen table, unevenly distributed yet also with a "just rightness" that is not imposed from without but rather is expressive of life at this time and place.

In ethics, then, Zen does not seek perfection or holiness insofar as these ideals are expressions of balance and regularity. Rather, Zen ethics manifest an inconsistency in behavior when that is called for and a consistency when that is demanded. One time and place and situation with just so many personal resources at hand call for one action. Another time and place and situation with other resources call for another behavior. The two actions do not necessarily have to fit together in a well-ordered pattern. Consistency and symmetry are not the rule. But neither are inconsistency and asymmetry the rule. Zen is neither bound by rules nor is it antinomian. Rather behavior is appropriate insofar as it is derived from life rather than imposed on life.

Such a style of life does not mean that life is unstructured or formless. Rather, people have developed a pattern of response and behavior that they bring with them into life situations as part of their resources. Sometimes that pattern will fit. At other times, it must be changed, better to fit the circumstances. A rigid imposition of a pattern on life is legalism. To have no pattern at all would be antinomian. To live a Zen life means to have a pattern but not to be bound by that pattern. A better way to express this might be: Zen involves bringing one's resources to an event but not to be bound by those resources. Surprising events can then take place!

2. Simplicity

Simplicity in art is the characteristic of sparseness, unobtrusiveness, being uncluttered, naiveté and abandon. Imagine a desert with very few trees or a green mountain in the distance or the sea from the beach or an unclouded sky. They are obviously sparse and uncluttered. They are simple. But we must not stop here. Zen simplicity has another important dimension. The feeling that the desert or sea or sky provokes is one of "boundlessness" or "limitlessness." It is in this sense that Zen art involves abandon or unrestraint. At the same time, however, there is the quality of unobtrusiveness. The Zen artist is not bound to any one form of life that must be portrayed. Rather life is as boundless as the sky and as bound as the forest. But neither the sky nor the forest is the rule. Rather the forest and sky mesh. The forest may be a boundary until one sees the sky. The sky may be overwhelming until one perceives the forest. The painting or bowl is uncluttered. It does not portray too much nor does it express too little. It may be a single branch against the sky with a love bird swinging on it in the breeze. Or it may be the lushness of a Japanese garden where the scarce space is all used appropriately. In both, nothing intrudes. Nothing imposes. Nothing pushes.

In ethics simplicity is characteristic of a life that is uncluttered or unadorned or austere. Such a quality must not be understood quantitatively. Simplicity of life does not depend on how much or how little a person owns or uses. A person who lived in a bare cell or a hobo could live a very complicated life. On the other hand an executive of a large firm could lead a simple life. What, then, is essential for simplicity?

The simple life, a life that is uncluttered and sparse, is a life in which objects and patterns and commitments and responsibilities are not binding or limiting of life. They are like the banks of a river that are the form of the river's flow. These banks do not confine the river. They can change. So also, the objects, patterns, commitments and responsibilities of a person's life can be felt to be binding when they clutter, when they are not experienced in relation to the whole of life as a mountain or forest will be experienced as massive while on it or in it, and as beautiful when seen in the midst of a semiarid land or against the sky. A simple life may contain the most complicated matters. It remains simple insofar as those matters do not impose or obtrude themselves out of a context. Thus, if I own an automobile, that object can be freeing or it can be a burden. When it is freeing, life can be experienced as uncluttered and simple. The automobile is then unobtrusive. It doesn't get in the way. Life is simple.

I am reminded of the Taoist story of a butcher who never sharpened his knife. When asked by his customers why, he responded that he knew where the spaces in the meat were. Hence, when he cut the meat, he encountered no opposition. A person who lives a simple life knows where the spaces are. This is Zen; it is a characteristic of a Zen ethic.

3. Austere Sublimity of Lofty Dryness

One can begin to intuit this characteristic of Zen aesthetics by imagining an old pine tree that is quite seasoned. That tree has sturdy boughs that have lost their greenness and youthfulness in the buffeting of many storms. Only the essence or the core remains. I am also reminded of some of the rock formations in northern Arizona and southern Utah. They are barren protrusions out of a dry earth, austere and stark, to say the least. Yet they also lift the human spirit with their redness and natural form. They stand out and yet do not obtrude. They are the essence of earth.

In the art of life this aesthetic character of Zen art is depicted in a mature, skillful, experienced behavior. The behavior is mature or seasoned. This does not mean that it is always the same. It is skillful but this does not necessarily mean that the person is an "expert." Rather what is done is not overdone or underdone. A speaker, e.g., would say only what needs to be said. Not a word more, not a word less! The speech points to the pith or core or essence. The action of care for another is just right. If too much is done for the others, they might feel smothered. If too little is done, they might be frustrated. To act or care with austere sublimity is to do only what needs to be done and not to do what is not called for.

4. Naturalness

In Zen, natural is not simply the opposite of artificial. A natural activity is one in which the actor is unstrained and not bound by intent. A poet, for example, may follow a seemingly artificial form of poetry such as haiku. The poem, however, is not squeezed into the form. Rather the poem finds itself in the form. The poet does not strain to fit an idea or feeling into the form but rather poet and form and idea or feeling come together in an unstrained and unintended manner. Intention, however, is not denied to the artist. Rather Zen naturalness negates "ordinary intention" in favor of a creative intent. Such creative intent is present "when the artist enters so thoroughly into what he is creating that no conscious effort, no distance between the two, remains."[15] The creative work and the artist are not one and not two. The total process is natural. It is unstrained and unselfconsciously realized.

When ethics is a series of principles to be imposed on life, human behavior is then artificial. This does not imply that Zen is wild or unprincipled. Many principles may be activated in the behavior. Rather when the principles are imposed without regard for the changes in the circumstances, then the behavior will not fit. On the other hand, if the behavior is merely whatever comes to mind at the moment, it also may not fit the situation. Zen naturalness of behavior happens when the person is relating directly to the life situation, and enters into it thoroughly and creatively. The action is then done, not by reason of conditioning or unintentionally. Rather the artist of life is conscious without strain and exhibits a pure and concentrated intention. Life is not made simply to fit into a precon- ceived and prefabricated form. At the same time, life is not left formless. The form fits the circumstances and the circumstances mold the form. The person is intrinsically and unselfconsciously in- volved, i.e., natural.

5. Subtle Profundity or Deep Reserve

Zen art is characterized by "reserve." This means that the art does not state baldly but rather "implies" or holds "within" itself that which it depicts. Not all is disclosed. This "implication" means that more can be perceived than is initially seen. The work of art is profound and subtle. It contains inexhaustible treasure. The subtle- ness of Zen art is not light but dark in its profundity. Darkness can be frightening or it can be calming. The darkness here is calm, paci- fying and still, restful and peaceful. Zen art is also stable, a stability that in its darkness is massive wherein a reverberation occurs. The echo resounds from a bottomless depth. Zen art is never totally dis- closing. It is open, yet it also retains a stability. Both its inexhaust- ibility and its rootedness effect peace and calm.

Many people desire closure in the art of living. It can become frustrating if some project is left unfinished and no possibility of completion is available. It would seem that the "subtle profundity" of Zen art would deprive life of such closure. The issue is, however, not the closure itself but rather the stability that can come with clo- sure. Here the Zen art of living is manifest in activity or behavior that is reserved or not entirely "out front," that is, "open-ended" behavior or behavior that does not close all possible avenues of fur- ther activity, behavior that arises from an inexhaustible source. At the same time the behavior is not anxious or tense or restless or in- secure. It is easy and tranquil, arising from the depth and always pointing beyond itself while being precisely itself and nothing more or less.

6. Freedom From Attachment

This quality of Zen art is often discussed in Zen literature as "nonattachment." It means "freedom from habit, convention, cus- tom, formula, rule, etc.—that is, not being bound to things."[16] Re- ality, for the Zen Buddhist, is impermanent. It is ever changing, ever in motion. The artist would seem to grasp a moment and to fix it. Habits, conventions, customs and formulas are attempts to form or structure reality. Zen does not object to structure. Rather, Zen always sees the impermanence of structure. Zen art is not bound by any rules or forms. The artist is not even bound by the characteristics described in this article. The Zen artist works with form and structure, creates it in such a way that it manifests reality and lets it go when it does not fit reality.

The Zen artist of life is free or unattached. This does not mean that this person is unreliable or inconsistent or irresponsible. We saw above, in the section on asymmetry, how the artist of life can be both consistent and inconsistent. Rather this artist is deeply responsible by being intimately involved in reality, immediately or directly involved. Such involvement calls for a profound responsibility in which, e.g., the Zen artist of life hears another as if he were himself. At the same time, however, the event or relation is not fixed. It is left open-ended. The artist of life is nonpossessive. The dynamics of freedom are like the movements of a river, always moving, never remaining in the same place, usually following a defined path but not confined to that path. The river changes when it must. It is not confined to one absolute form. It is alive.

A Zen ethic is, at root, an ethic of nonattachment or freedom. To be free is to be enlightened. Each human person is cast into this world at a time and place, none of which is chosen. That person is then socialized into the forms of a particular culture, forms such as language, behavior patterns, structures of perception. The Zen artist of life cannot and does not deny these forms. Rather the forms are not binding. The artist of life changes like the wind, able to assume the forms it meets and to discard them when they are inappropriate. That person is free or, as designated in Zen, a "man of no title." The Zen artist of life is not confined to any form yet is open to any form, is unable to be defined yet open to any definition, has plumbed inexhaustible depths yet still lives on the surface, is not bound by any title or name or description yet able to take on any title. The Zen artist of life walks with a sure foot but leaves no footprints. Such a style is manifest in the images of a few lines in the Jewish Book of Proverbs (30:18–19):

> Three things are wonderful for me
> Yes, four I cannot understand:
> The way of an eagle in the air,
> The way of a serpent upon a rock,
> The way of a ship on the high seas,
> The way of a man with a maiden.

The eagle and the serpent and the ship ultimately leave no traces (I don't know why the "man with a maiden" is grouped here!).

In Zen, the quality of freedom or nonattachment is also the root of respect for all living creatures and for the *mahakaruna* (great love) of the Bodhisattva. To respect and be compassionate involves an openness of mind and heart to be able to receive the other or to enter into the life of the other, to take on their forms. It is to do this nonpossessively (leaving no tracks behind) and yet with profound appreciation and care, or love. This is an ethical artistry that is almost unequaled throughout the world yet able to be realized anywhere or anytime.

7. Tranquility

In Zen art, the quality of tranquility is not manifested by way of passivity or inactivity. To be tranquil is to be "composed" and calm. Composure involves an inner centeredness that does not deny outward sensitivity. To be composed is to be "all together" or congruent. Tranquility is not simply a restful calm. It is rather a composure that exists in the midst of motion, an activity in the midst of quiet and a quiet in the midst of activity. D. T. Suzuki expresses this when he writes:

> Zen takes hold of life in its wholeness and moves "restlessly" with it or stays quietly with it. Wherever there is any sign of life at all, there is Zen. When, however, the "eternal tranquility" is abstracted from "the restless movement on the surface of life," it sinks into death, and there is no more of the surface either. The tranquility of Zen is in the midst of "the boiling oil," the surging waves. . . .[17]

Zen tranquility is alive. It is a quality of life taken as a whole rather than piecemeal. It is not a state or condition taken out of life as, e.g., in a monastic cell. Rather it is a dimension of life along with restlessness.

Just as Zen art is characterized as tranquil, so also the Zen artist of life is tranquil. Tranquility, as an ethical mode, is not passivity or quietism or indifference or inactivity. It is rather a quality of life manifest in the behavior of a person whether the person is active or quiet. Thus there can be anxious passivity or anxious activity as well as a calm, composed activity or passivity. A calm person is not necessarily a passive person nor is calmness a zombie-like reserve. Tranquility is not a tranquilizer. The tranquil person is very aware and alive. I once heard a story from Bernard Phillips about an incident between himself and the roshi of a Zen monastery where he resided while in Japan. One morning Bernard did something that deeply angered the roshi who immediately told Bernard what he thought and felt. Such a feeling might seem to be the opposite of tranquility. Immediately afterward (I was about to say "when he calmed down"), the roshi invited Bernard to visit some Buddhist temples with him. The anger was completely gone. This anecdote leads me to suggest that Zen tranquility is not the opposite of anxiety but rather a quality of a person in whom no feeling or circumstance can rule the person. Thus a tranquil person can feel anxiety or fear or anger or passion or excitement or joy or anticipation but no one of these feelings or any other feeling will so rule the person that they are "out of control." Such a person is composed. As Suzuki suggests, he or she "takes hold of life in its wholeness and moves 'restlessly' with it or stays quietly with it."

Conclusion

A Zen painting does not exhibit only one or a few of these seven characteristics. Rather, all are present in the painting. The same is true of the Zen artist of life. No characteristic is independent of any of the others. All intertwine in the everchanging fabric of life. Furthermore, the Zen artist of life is both painter and painting, creator and object of creation. It is life that is being created and the artist of life is not separate from life but part of its dynamic flow. The Zen artist of life and, hence, the Zen ethic is like the wind that is shaped symmetrically or asymmetrically, unobtrusive yet also felt, boundless yet confined, just what it is and natural, obvious yet mysterious, trackless and tranquil, calm and restless. Each of these qualities forms a complex that can penetrate every aspect of life from culture to art to the daily life of people. In fact, culture and art are the daily life. It is in a person's style of life that an ethic is manifest. Zen conceives of itself as the root source of any style. No style can be called simply Zen. Thus these characteristics do not give us a Zen ethic but point to a Zen of ethics.

Notes

1. D. T. Suzuki, *Zen and Japanese Culture* (Princeton, N.J.: Princeton University Press, 1970), p. 27.
2. D. T. Suzuki, *An Introduction to Zen* (N.Y.: Grove, 1964), p. 130.
3. *Ibid.*, p. 64.
4. D. T. Suzuki, E. Fromm, and R. DeMartino, *Zen Buddhism and Psychoanalysis* (N.Y.: Grove, 1960), p. 16.
5. My primary sources for this discussion will be D. T. Suzuki and

Shin'ichi Hisamatsu. In my estimation, they are the most reliable witnesses of Zen in a Western language.

6. D. T. Suzuki, *An Introduction to Zen*, p. 37.

7. Cf. D. T. Suzuki, *Essays in Zen Buddhism, First Series* (N.Y.: Grove, 1949), pp. 54, 357.

8. Shin'ichi Hisamatsu. "Zen: Its Meaning for Modern Civilization," *The Eastern Buddhist*, New Series, 1, 1 (Sept., 1965), p. 22.

9. Cf. D. T. Suzuki, *Zen and Japanese Culture*, p. 44.

10. D. T. Suzuki, *Zen Buddhism*, ed. by William Barrett (N.Y.: Doubleday, 1956), p. 259.

11. D. T. Suzuki, *An Introduction to Zen*, p. 64.

12. *Ibid.*

13. *Ibid.*

14. S. Hisamatsu, *Zen and the Fine Arts* (Palo Alto: Kodansha, 1971), pp. 28–38. The remainder of this article will contain a summary of these pages in which Hisamatsu describes the characteristics of Zen art. This will then be followed, in each case, with my translation of these characteristics into an ethic.

15. *Ibid.*, p. 32.

16. *Ibid.*, p. 34.

17. D. T. Suzuki, *Zen and Japanese Culture*, p. 356.

Benevolence:
Confucian Ethics and Ecstasy

Thaddeus J. Gurdak

The Confucian tradition, precisely because it is a disjointed tradition of some twenty-five hundred years' duration, often provides its interpreters with seemingly insurmountable problems of exegesis and explication. Even though it is customary to speak of *a* Confucian tradition, there are, nevertheless, at least two distinct streams of development: one following the lineage of Hsün Tzu (third century B.C.) through Chu Hsi of the Sung dynasty, the other following the lineage of Mencius (fourth century B.C.) through Wang Yang-ming of the Ming dynasty. In the tradition of Hsün Tzu *li*, ritual-propriety, was considered the central virtue. That tradition undertook the correction of a human nature predisposed to do wrong by enforcing strict standards of adherence to discipline. The Mencian tradition, on the other hand, emphasized man's essential goodness and his capacity for development through self-examination and the practice of social virtues. The Mencian tradition, is the tradition of *jen*, benevolence. These traditions furthermore, did not develop in any orderly or organic manner: each was promulgated as the foundation of a national orthodoxy, sometimes abruptly accepted, infallibly decreed, and adamantly propagated until its abrupt rejection or reinterpretation by a new dynasty. While one tradition was in ascendance, the other did not die: it survived either in exile, or openly as loyal opposition, and at times was even able to insinuate itself into the fabric of the reigning orthodoxy, creating thereby a unique blend of perspective. This intellectual hopscotching through history notwithstanding, Confucianism has succeeded in establishing itself as integral to the very spirit of the Chinese people. At the same time this pattern of acceptance and rejection has made the task of tracing the tradition to its sources in Confucius's own teaching very difficult.

A number of classical texts are available that claim to record the very words of the Master himself, but careful literary criticism has shown that these texts, among them *The Doctrine of the Mean, The Great Learning, The Book of Rites,* and *The School Sayings of Confucius,* are products of later orthodoxies and the debates between these orthodoxies: none can be trusted to reflect clearly the original teaching of Confucius or of the earliest stratum of Confucian teaching. Only the *Lun-yü, The Analects,* remains as a likely source for an understanding of the Master's thought, but even the *Lun-yü* is not without its problems. It is a text of late compilation, at least five generations removed from Confucius, the work of an unknown compiler that shows no discernible theme of compilation. Internal consistencies show it to be a collectaneum of smaller collectanea, added to by any number of hands, some of which were more than likely non-Confucian.

There is some consensus concerning which of the twenty books of *The Analects* are the oldest and are therefore reflective of the earliest stratum of Confucian teaching. Arthur Waley cites Books III–IX as representative of that oldest stratum,[1] while Professor Ch'ien Mu writes that Books I–X may be so accepted.[2] For this inquiry Waley's thesis will be accepted, but those portions of Books I and II that show similarities of style, construction, and intent to Books III to IX will also be consulted.[3]

Having thus delineated the meager resources available for our study, we turn our attention to the task at hand, the attempt to describe or to define, according to the earliest stratum of Confucian thought, the significance of the virtue *jen,* benevolence. The longstanding debate concerning the proper translation of the term cannot be discussed. Whether Waley's translation, "goodness," or Helmut Wilhelm's "humanheartedness," or the more traditional "benevolence" of James Legge is used, each must be seen as a convention rather than a translation. No single English word can fully circumscribe its significance.

Of primary importance to this task is the initial understanding that benevolence is not an acquired virtue, earned by adherence to certain patterns of behavior or attitudinal development. It is, rather, a quality of being which has its roots in the very heart of a person[4] and which is given expression in the totality of one's life of interrelationship. Etymologically, the structure of the graph may well be derived from the symbol for man and the symbol for pluralization, denoting therefore the quality of relationality between persons,[5] or that quality or qualities common to the community of men in relationship. Its situation at the heart of human personhood is expressed even by its similarity of pronunciation to the word "man", both of which were pronounced *ńźien*.

Confucius never claimed to be a systematic philosopher. Consequently, *The Analects* contain no definitions, analogies, or theoretical descriptions of benevolence itself. Confucius is portrayed, rather, as using the term in instruction without making a theoretical understanding of benevolence the content of instruction. It is, therefore, to the context of Confucian learning, to the relationship between teacher and student, that one must turn to begin a search for the significance of benevolence.

Confucius says concerning his favorite disciple, Yen Hui:

> The Master said: "Incomparable, indeed, is Hui. A small portion of rice, a gourd of water, living on a lowly street— others would find it unendurably depressing, but such an experience makes no difference to Hui's cheerfulness. Hui is indeed incomparable."
>
> *(Analects VI.9)*[6]

> "Hui is capable of occupying his mind for three months on end with no thought other than benevolence. The others (disciples) can do so, some for a day, some for a month, but that is all."
>
> *(Analects VII. 5)*

It is of this same disciple that Confucius is reputed to have declared, "Hui is not far from it."[7] "It" is here taken traditionally to mean benevolence. Thus, the quality of benevolence is not changed by circumstance. Hui is one who in the face of poverty, mean circumstance, or nonacceptance remains with his heart still set on the Way as taught by his master. His life reflects a central core of stability, a reflection of his grasp of an ultimacy of meaning not capable of destruction or diminution.

> "The gentleman (*chün-tzu*) who parts company with benevolence is not worthy of the name. Never does a gentleman leave the way of benevolence, nor is he ever so busy or so weak that he can no longer grasp it."
>
> *(Analects IV.5)*

Benevolence is the ultimate concern of the Confucian gentleman. Ultimacy of concern, however, is not a self-validating reality, for ultimacy of concern or even tenacity of concern does not guarantee that the given concern is reflective of the reality of the Ultimate: it does not guarantee that the concern cannot be or become no more than an exercise in solipsistic self-deception. The health of one's ultimate concern is validated by its fruits. When the existential focus of concern coincides with the ontology of Ultimacy (in Confucius's vision, with the will of Heaven and with the sacred Tradition which expresses that will), then life can continue positively and cheerfully, with continuing commitment to the Way of concern even in the face of straitened circumstance. External circumstance notwithstanding, the individual lives in the conviction that he is in touch with a sense of meaning that would not otherwise be his.

Confucius is reputed to have said of himself:

"At fifteen years of age, I committed myself to study; at thirty, I was firm in my resolve; at forty, I suffered from no more doubt; at fifty, I knew the Will of Heaven; at sixty, I heard its dictates with a compliant ear; at seventy, I followed my own heart for what I desired no longer overstepped the boundary of what is right."

(Analects II.4)

This passage, with its striking resemblance to the Thomistic understanding of great freedom, that is, the freedom always to do the good (written some seventeen hundred years before the time of the Angelic Doctor), expresses most lucidly this quality of personal stability in obedience and truth. Truth comes from Heaven and is received through a vigorous and unrelenting process of study. After being heard, it is to be obeyed, but obedience eventually gives way to the development of a character so molded in accordance with that truth that the individual will and the heavenly will come to exist in harmony. The one becomes expressive of the other, the other of the one, so that the will of Heaven becomes the will of the individual. In this paradigmatic attitudinal history Confucius is presented as a model of the stability of conviction and truth that is received from Ultimacy itself through a faithful study of the Way of the ancient Fathers.

This state of existence, the conviction and certainty of meaning, is a state Paul Tillich terms ecstasy. The term has unfortunately been saddled with a series of connotations all related to an overabundance of emotion within religious experience and perception. Ecstasy, however, Tillich writes, "must be rescued from its distorted connotations and be restored to a sober theological function.

If this proves to be impossible, the reality which is described by the word will disappear from our sight unless another word can be found."[8]

> Ecstasy ('standing outside one's self') points to a state of mind which is extraordinary in the sense that the mind transcends its ordinary situation. Ecstasy is not a negation of reason; it is a state of mind in which reason is beyond itself, that is, beyond its subject-object structure. In being beyond itself, reason does not deny itself. "Ecstatic reason" remains reason: it does not receive anything irrational or antirational—which it could not do without self-destruction—but it transcends the basic condition of finite rationality, the subject-object structure.[9]

Thus to attribute ecstasy to either Confucius or his disciples is in no wise to accuse them of enthusiasm, emotionalism, shamanism, or of questing for altered states of consciousness. Their ecstasy was rather the verification, the validation of their focus of meaning in Ultimacy itself. These men have found a vision, a commitment, a wisdom so clear that the pleasure of living within its reality does not depart from them. It is the world itself that sets the state of ecstasy at odds with the expression of ecstasy. Yen Hui's cheerfulness, the tenacity of a true gentleman's hold on the Way are strange because the surrounding society is no longer grounded in Ultimacy through the Way. As the guardian of the frontier mound at I[10] stated: "It is now a very long time since the Way prevailed in the world."[11]

Confucius was well aware of the tension that existed between ecstatic wisdom and the wisdom of the society that judged his way to be folly.

> The Master said: "Ning Wu-tzu, so long as the Way prevailed in his country was a very wise man: but when the Way no longer prevailed, he was a fool. His wisdom is capable of emulation, but few, if any, can emulate his folly."
>
> (*Analects* V.20)

Ning Wu-tzu was an officer in the state of Wei under Duke Wen (ruled 660–635 B.C.). In the first part of the term of his office the state was quiet and prosperous and Ning "wisely acquitted himself of his duties."[12] Later, his duke was overthrown and incarcerated, yet Ning's devotion and loyalty remained exemplary: he continued to care for Wen while he was in prison, even to the point of sending him food through a bamboo tube.[13] His loyalty was vindicated when he saw the restoration of his prince to his rightful throne.[14] Many, Confucius comments, can emulate Ning's wisdom in peace and prosperity, but few can be so convinced of their vision and commitment that they can live it when others judge it to be folly.[15] Only the strongest of persons can live a life different from that of the rest of society without that society's approval or reinforcement. In most cases peer pressure, either open or subliminal, will bring about the gradual diminution of the individual's meaning structure, resulting in accommodation, acculturation, and finally the submission of the individual to the group.

It is precisely at this point that the importance of ritual-propriety, *li*, to the Confucian world view becomes apparent. Confucius was a teacher of ritual. He instructed his students in all manner of deportment as it was to be practiced in all human interrelationship. Since it was by Heaven's leave and under Heaven's watchful eye that the dynasty continued in existence, all human activity was understood, therefore, to stand under the aegis of Heaven's mandate. Man's proper response was reverence and awe. All human life, because it was willed by Heaven, participated in the very reality of transcendence. Human life became liturgy. One's relationships with family, friends, and colleagues, one's relationships at court, and one's participation in the state ritual of prayer and sacrifice all expressed and reinforced the contiguity of the human with the Ultimate.

The group that gathers in commemoration at a royal sacrifice constitutes a community, one committed to the ideas, ideals, and the meaning structure given form in the ritual itself. Each repetition of the ritual further intensifies the lessons of the ritual, validating the meaning structure therein, allowing the participants to carry with them that meaning, in opposition if necessary, to the society around them, until such time as the structure can again be validated liturgically, or until the society as a whole accepts the meaning structure expressed in the liturgy. For Confucius the wisdom, the meaning he sought to express and to live was found in the Ways of the Ancients. Contemporary society no longer reflected that Way. Thus, through education—particularly through education in ritual—he preserved and transmitted that wisdom which was, in turn, to be lived and preserved by his students. The validation of Confucian wisdom was to be found in the continuing communal celebration and individual commitment to the Ways of the Ancients in a society whose goals and aspirations had strayed from the true source of all truth.

In liturgical ritual the community of the kingdom recalls its past, and through the act of recalling brings to conscious appreciation the relationship established by Heaven between itself and the kingdom. The liturgical ritual is the locus of all effectual transformation of human perception from that of its own wisdom to that wisdom which is given from above: it is the focus of ultimacy for the people. Peter Berger writes:

> They [religious acts and legitimations] restore ever again the continuity between the present moment and the social tradition, placing the experiences of the individual and the various groups of that society in the context of a history that transcends them all. It has been rightly said that society, in its essence, is a memory. It may be added that, through most of human history, this memory has been a religious one.[16]

As the focus of ultimacy the actions of the rite become paradigms for royal and ministerial governance, and provide that structure of reality that gives meaning to loyalty and obedience. In the actualization of relationality the conferral of the divine mandate is accomplished as it was done in the beginning, *in illo tempore*. The *Shang-shu, The Book of Documents,* a text known to be used by Confucius in the instruction of his students (although it is not yet known which books of the present redactions he had access to) states:

> In our two states order was created, and our Western territories relied on him (King Wen). This was seen and heard by God-on-high, and God showed him favor. Heaven resolutely ordered Wen to destroy the Yin (the Shang Dynasty) and to receive its mandate: (He accomplished this) and the states and the people became orderly.[17]

The doctrine of the Mandate of Heaven teaches that the kingship is conferred only on those who have proven their virtue, and on those who by their righteousness and justice rule for the sake of the common good. It was generally understood that as soon as a king lost sight of his status as a servant-ruler, as did the kings of

Yin, his right to rule was withdrawn by Heaven and given to one more worthy of the responsibility. Here again, relationality, and particularly a relationality in which one is primarily concerned with the good of another, assumes the role of ethical ideal. This relationship is the source of the virtue of benevolence, and its practice by the Ancients stands as its principal paradigm.

China in the age of Confucius no longer followed the Way of the Ancients. Strife, warfare, profiteering, nepotism, and treachery were rampant among the states and statelets of feudal China in the last years of the Chou ascendancy. This situation was the source, it seems, of Confucius's living on the brink of despair. Yet he understood that there was a transcendent foundation which, although lost at present, would be recovered in the lives of his students individually and as they contributed to the next generation of governmental functionaries.

> Someone asked for an explanation of the *Ti* (Ancestral) sacrifice. The Master said: "I don't know: but anyone who did know could do all things under Heaven as easily as I do this." He put his finger into the palm of his hand.
>
> *(Analects* III.11)

In the rites one came to know the reality of one's relationship with the transcendent and of one's relationship with one's fellow-men through the transcendent. One came to appreciate and to accept the demands that transcendence made on the ruler, the minister, and the commoner alike. In the ecstasy of liturgical reality one knew and accepted the moral imperative of benevolence.

There would be days, however, when the state could no longer be trusted to preserve the liturgy and to act in accordance with its dictates. There would be days when liturgy would be little more than vacuous pomp and circumstance or a petty political showpiece.[18] There would be days when the severity of Heaven's judgment would be forgotten. In times such as these the responsibility for the preservation of the Ways of the Ancients would fall to the individual. By the study of the ancient texts, *The Book of Documents* and the *Book of Songs,* and by self-examination, the individual would take upon himself the burden of being the historical remembrance of the community. He would be for the community the living reminder of its past and the paradigm of its present: he would be its teacher. He would stand in recognition of the demand of Heaven in the sacrality of human existence and therein give of himself for the common good. He would live in poverty and mean circumstance, yet have no thought in his mind other than benevolence.

Notes

1. Arthur Waley, *The Analects of Confucius* (New York: Random House–Vintage Books, n.d., c. 1938), p. 21.

2. Ch'ien Mu, *Lun-yü yao-lüeh* (Taipei: The Commercial Press, 1964), pp. 8–9.

3. Book X poses a distinct problem by reason of its difference in style and subject matter from the rest of *The Analects*. Instead of being concerned with the basic principles of Confucian wisdom, Book X records students' remembrances of the minutiae of the Master's ritual behavior. Waley rejects its authenticity; Ch'ien accepts it. While this writer is inclined to accept Ch'ien's arguments, a full presentation of these difficulties is unnecessary since none of the material of the book concerns the matters here under discussion.

4. Ch'ien Mu, *Lun-yü hsin-chieh* (Hong Kong: New Asia Institute of Graduate Study, 1964), p. 252.

5. Bernhard Karlgren, *Analytic Dictionary of Chinese and Sino-Japanese* (New York: Dover Publications, 1974), p. 271, no. 930.

6. These comments on the character of Yen Hui are restructured into general principles in *Analects* IV.9 and VII.15.

7. *Analects* XI.18.

8. Paul Tillich, *Systematic Theology*, 3 vols. (Chicago: University of Chicago Press, 1951–1963), 1:111.

9. *Ibid.*, 1:111–112.

10. I was the boundary marker between Lu (Confucius' state) and the state of Wei. See Waley, *Analects*, p. 100, note 6.

11. *Analects* III.24.

12. James Legge, translator. *The Confucian Analects* (New York: Dover Publications, 1971), p. 180.

13. Waley, *Analects*, p. 112, note 5.

14. Legge, *Analects*, p. 181.

15. The text reads that Ning's folly cannot be emulated, a rhetorical overstatement. Confucius is pessimistic in his assessment of how many can attain the ideal, but the ideal is not impossible. Our translation of the text, therefore, softens the overstatement.

16. Peter Berger, *The Sacred Canopy: Elements of a Sociological Theory of Religion* (Garden City, N.Y.: Doubleday and Company, 1969), p. 41.

17. *K'ang Kao*, 4. Bernhard Karlgren, translator. *The Book of Documents* (Stockholm: The Museum of Far Eastern Antiquities, 1950), p. 39. This chapter is one accepted by all scholars as being the product of Chou dynasty authorship.

18. See *Analects* III.1–2, 5–6.

Applying Comparative Ethics to Multinational Corporations

Roderick Hindery

Like the first blinding flashes of massive nuclear energy at White Sands, New Mexico, and Hiroshima, the explosive, exponential growth of multinational enterprises or corporations (MNCs) since 1945 blinds the human imagination. Shallow and proliferating overcoverage by the media raises human consciousness of MNCs less than it cultivates an illusory sense of cozy familiarity and security. So dramatic are the ethical and other problems raised by MNCs that within a few lines they can only be suggested. A preliminary reference to the immensity, electronic computer speed, and ongoing, geometrically accelerating expansion of MNCs may indicate their incredible impact on present and future prospects for human survival and international cooperation.

United States based MNCs alone already rank as the third largest economic force in the world after the U.S. and the U.S.S.R. Of the top fifty MNCs, twenty-seven are parented in countries other than the U.S. or the U.S.S.R., like the Netherlands, the United Kingdom, Iran, Japan, and Germany.[1] Profiles of U.S. and "foreign"-based MNCs generally exclude nonindustrial transnational corporations like A.T.& T. whose economic muscle and influence appear to be equally formidable, exhilarating, or both, depending on one's point of view. The thirteen largest U.S.-based transnational banks—like Citicorp and Bankamerica Corporation—experienced, by my computation, an average annual growth in foreign earnings from 1970–1975 of nearly 50 percent.[2]

The underlying inference is that the total enormity and might of U.S. and foreign industrial and nonindustrial multinational enterprises vies immeasurably with the economic and related political strength of all nation-states combined. The geometrically quickening growth of MNCs is partly divulged by the fact that the 500 top U.S. industrials *doubled* their gross and net incomes in the five years previous to 1978.[3] General Motors alone holds the economic clout of the world's fifteenth most powerful nation-state, Belgium. Exxon corresponds to Denmark, General Electric to Greece, and IBM to Norway and Portugal.[4]

The immensity, the accelerating velocity of management and expansion, and the power of MNCs, in their individual and social ethical ramifications, affect most issues that were once considered within the insular ambits of a single nation, culture, or religious tradition. One can no longer intelligibly converse about human rights and responsibilities—like economic and derivative political, ecological, and cultural interactions—without an international, cross-cultural, and comparative ethical perspective.

MNCs force the following contemporary assessment of the discipline of ethics: ethics is necessarily comparative. This is a pragmatic fact of life long obscured by provincially Western, pseudo-Christian and pseudo-Catholic philosophical frameworks for moral reflection and decision. The phenomenon of MNCs, to which Part II below will relate comparative ethical analyses, now reveals the preposterous futility of ignoring ethics in its comparative dimension. Previous to the application of comparative ethics to MNCs, a preliminary résumé will review the meaning of the belatedly new field of comparative ethics.

I. The Meaning, Criteria, and Limits of Comparative Ethics

In one sense Western ethical thought has always proceeded comparatively as it cross-examined continuities and disparities in the many historical layers of, for example, Christian moral systems. This cross-examination was naturally extended to the many subtraditions of Christianity in general and to further subdivisions of each Christian tradition in particular, say Roman Catholic tradition.

At the surface the evaluative categories were foundational norms like the golden rule, middle or more proximate norms with exceptions, and the religious and/or human grounds for both. The correlating criteria also comprised virtues, vices, rights, and responsibilities. In a recent book and other publications on comparative ethics I have attempted to clarify and reorganize these conventional, age-old queries into five sets of comparative criteria.[5] I have further extended them to a less provincial and more fully human cross-cultural sphere. The first three interrogations are substantive: *what* do you claim to know? The last two comparative criteria are epistemological: *how* do you ground a moral truth-claim? That is, what are the ultimate and proximate sources of your moral "knowledge"?

1. *Morality or mores?* Does an ethical affirmation touch moral choice or mere convention? The answer lies in the custom's origin, goals, and universality. Take the legitimation of a profit like 12 to 15 percent annual interest. Did it originate freely or by force inflicted on one or more of the parties concerned? Was its goal the isolated, profiteering welfare of one, or the welfare of an individual or group combined with that of others? Was the justification of high interest universally applied to every party in exactly the same circumstances? Or did the factors of power, heredity, and class replace equity with discrimination? When some people allege that MNCs affect not morality but mores, that they involve amoral matters of convention, their assertion can be tested in the light of their personal gains and apparent motives as well as the personal effects that MNCs have on individuals and societies.

2. *What ethos is salient in moral systems?* An ethos may refer to a specific value, virtue, or cluster of virtues, like Max Weber's so-called Protestant ethic or ethos of thrift and hard work—an ethos he related to the genesis of capitalism. Ethos may also connote the grounds and goals of those values and virtues such as a) resignation to competitive or even predatory patterns of human, economic behavior and b) aspiration for worldly success as a sign of divine election. Further, ethos signals the emotive atmosphere, affective élan, and magnetic attraction of a moral emphasis, like British perseverance or Italian *joie de vivre*. Lastly, ethos evokes the uniqueness or specificity of given moral systems, even if some of their norms are considered cross-cultural in historical fact or as a precondition for human survival. A grasp of ethos is vital for comprehending the milieu in which MNCs and their personnel formulate moral decisions.

3. *What primal convictions prevail about the relationships between individuals and societal conventions or institutions?* Do societies or corporations like MNCs discriminate against economic and other human rights on the bases of relative individual weaknesses, race, sex, age, appearance, religion or heredity? Conversely, in what ways, if any, do individuals recognize responsibilities to contribute socially to their compatriots or corporations? In what manner do they not only ask what their country or MNC can do for them?

4. The fourth basis of ethical evaluation is less substantive than epistemological: *what are the ultimate sources of moral valuing?* In the present context this question demands special elaboration. Generally, people validate their assertions by pointing to an interrelated composite of direct experiences or felt values that are allegedly religious or intuitively moral. Direct ethical appeals to experience are exemplified in proclamations about the obvious sanctity of human life or the self-evident worth of persons that is not to be wholly identified with their economic or social productivity.

At a more reflective, second order, or indirect level of experience, people strive to justify moral declarations by calling on various forms of collective experience. At a comparably indirect level, they *reason* from the beneficent and problematic consequences of their individual behavior or of planned structures, like MNCs, by which behavior is largely influenced. While experiential allegations are said to be variously direct and foundational or indirect and reflective, their species are far more variegated than the few listed above. For instance, East Asians, among others, feel that ethical truth-claims are inseparable from esthetic awareness. Others like Daniel Maguire have linked moral consciousness to sensitivities for the comic, tragic, and creative imagination of moral alternatives.[6] Religious and philosophical traditions have referred the wellsprings of ethical knowledge and judgment to dozens of human virtues or qualities that expand human character and moral insight.

Solid ethical discernment compares, assesses, and orchestrates the input of these quite multiple resources of moral consciousness.[7] The secret of accurate moral decision lies in grasping the interrelatedness of various fonts of ethical knowledge. Thus, *at its epistemological roots, moral judgment is intrinsically comparative.* Its breadth is not parochial or elitist insofar as it does not overemphasize a single source, such as written traditions or isolated reasoning (rationalism). Instead the scope of ethics is cosmopolitan. It addresses itself in nonelitist style to the professional wisdoms of religious, philosophical, or economical leaders, but also to the systemic insights of populist traditions. Many so-called common people are "lovers of wisdom (philosophers)" whose axioms, art, and folklore are ignored only at the peril of glorifying systematic reflection as an exclusive oracle. In Chinese tradition "Everyman" is meant to be a sage. Elitist monopolies or wisdom is not identified with aristocratic excellence. In theory aristocracy is extended to "everyman"—like the Christian Kingdom of God. Just as the cross-cultural phenomenon of MNCs affects the dual aristocracies of leaders and their communities, so it draws upon both of their varied sources of ethical wisdom.

5. *What are the mediate and proximate guides for moral judgment?* Some norms or maxims guide actions more proximately than do the principles that encapsulate ultimate moral sources and value-claims like the consciousness of human worth and the golden rule. These axioms range from mediate or middle maxims like "in doubt, presume in favor of the possessor" to working rules like "let the buyer or consumer beware," a maxim that may guide choice more proximately. Middle and proximate action-guides are not absolutes. Rather they are operative or prima facie presumptions that are sometimes overridden by other norms which also link into a given case.

In the context of comparative ethics it must be stressed first that the transfer-value of middle maxims diminishes in proportion to their concreteness. However, their cross-cultural reliability increases to the degree in which they embody general values accepted cross-culturally, like the love and justice articulated in broad principles such as the golden rule. In other words, the flexibility of middle maxims is proportionate to their concreteness. Thus the human ability to sense exceptions to rules correlates proportionately with one's feeling for a maxim's unique specificity.[8]

The critical sensitivity to proportionality or to what is fitting or due remains subject to the human factors of error and egoism. As a result middle maxims are abused, just as they are sometimes exploited for unjust goals. The axioms mentioned previously about possession and purchasing were once manipulated to defend excessive accumulation and profit. The norm about possession may be currently reapplied to favor the basic rights of lesser developed nations (LDCs). In conflicts of interest with MNCs about managerial control or about profits from resources, the presumption can be predicated in favor of the possessor (the LDC), even though it can be overridden in wider contexts of equity. In a comparable vein, "let the consumer beware" can function as the stimulus for programs of consumer education, including education about mutating strains of MNCs, their bewildering political and cultural impacts, and the variously human values they market.[9]

Three subsections now examine 1) the transfer value of ethical ideals and norms, 2) their moral limits, and 3) the performance gap in executing the fruits of comparative ethical analysis.

1. *The transfer value of ethical ideals and norms.* The initial task entails distinguishing values that are authentically cross-cul-

tural from their intra-cultural counterfeits. From my own research
and travels I have concluded that the golden rule of loving both self
and others is generally, if not universally, admired. In reverse proportion, egotism and its symbiotic twin, the death instinct, are as-
piringly disdained. On what warrants? As the celebrated senior
Confucian Mou Tsungsan rephrased Mencius for me: whoever does
not autonomously feel compassion for starving children and adults,
is, by definition, not human.[10] To feel otherwise is to abdicate either
to egotism or to heteronomous collective pressures, authorities, or
propaganda. Or, as the Hindu philosopher, Margaret Chatterjee, in-
formed me: the self-evidence of justice and love, either you see or
you do not. While these primordial moral declarations may not be
verifiable in the strictest sense, many believe that they can be partly substantiated through the comparative employment of multiple
ethical sources, like reason and collective experience.

Conversely, the same check-and-balance system discloses that
not all cultural values are equally cross-cultural. The United States
citizen cannot clone apparently productive Japanese economic and
moral values like social dependence and loyalty (amae and giri).[11]
These qualities are inexplicable apart from deep historical roots of
spartan, crowded, island existence and the interacting ethoses of
Japanese folk religions, Shinto, Bushido, Buddhism, and Confucianism. In a polar example, if the peoples of Hong Kong or Tokyo simply continue to parrot American styles of rock music, dress,
transportation, and beef consumption, they will bankrupt themselves economically and lose their cultural identity. These incipient
tragedies do not lack their moral dimensions.

2. *Moral limits: not all maxims are directly moral.* A second
qualification about the comparative value of middle axioms asserts
that not all of them are *directly* moral. True, the problematic consequences of MNCs on world starvation, poverty, or armament do affect individual persons and therefore entail a mélange of moral
implications. But the causes of those problems are not always directly moral or attributable, for instance, to the individual avarice
of specified corporate executives. Those who cavalierly project such
personal indictments on the integrity of others often tell the world
more about their own avarice or moralistic self-righteousness than
about the integrity of those whom they would judge. Matters that
require human praise and censure are not persons but their actions
and, above all, the structural systems by which their behavior is
largely programmed. Such systems are uniquely exemplified by the
increasingly complex diversity of mutating MNCs and their chain-
reacting consequences, both beneficent and destructive.

Granted the foregoing stipulations about middle rules, others can still be gathered that are indirectly moral. They are assembled by inductive trial and error. Abundant instances of constructive maxims that structurally and indirectly affect cooperative, moral relationships have been recently outlined by Richard H. Viola.[12] Other examples: 1) external accountability and public audit are indispensable for public services that are up front and effective, yet 2) without proper safeguards the product of audits can be manipulated for the partisan interests of competitive economic or political groups or by media that, for commercial purposes, intend to make news when there is no news.

Clarified middle rules and ultimate moral principles are as cross-culturally pervasive and practical as the fullness of Jewish justice,[13] Christian altruism, or Muslim abhorrence for idolatry. Other values are comparably universal, like Hindu Rigvedic life-affirmation, the Buddhist reverence that proscribes excessive desire and material consumption,[14] or the Confucian respect for youth and the elderly. In short, the theory and application of religious or humanistic ethics are not merely European or American. In its values and its norms ethics spans cultures and historical eras. While each moral system retains its specific ethos, value emphases, and norms, a commonality (catholicity with a small c) of ethics perdures. Absolutist moral relativism, which is self-contradictory, is finally yielding to a comparative, pluralistic ethics whose nucleus contains a relatively small list of intercultural human rights and responsibilities.

3. *The performance gap in executing the fruits of comparative ethical analysis.* Of course, the enshrinement of ideals in basic principles and middle maxims is not enough. They suffer a performance gap in Asia and elsewhere. Hindu and Christian middle rules about liberation and equality for all lag far behind the cultural and economic realities of class divisions. Beyond the comparative, clear application of values through moral principles and action guides, people also need inspiration. As the economist Gunnar Myrdal has proclaimed, human beings need live humanistic or spiritual leaders like Gandhi and Tagore to lead and galvanize their fellow human beings into moral action.

With the statement of these clarifications about the meaning, transfer value, and limits of comparative ethical criteria and maxims, this inquiry resumes its applied focus on international economics. The reason for the concentration on economics rests not only on the value-laden significance of MNCs in themselves. Rather, economics constitutes the most neglected key to solving correlated problems in other moral and social areas. Would that research in business ethics were financially endowed on scales comparable to other subjects like medical ethics. I shall not speculate here on the reasons why endowments for open-minded research on business ethics are relatively nonexistent. But at present, most of the prolific literature on business ethics, micro and macro, flows from the business community itself, not all of it philanthropic in effect.[15] In note 25 below I append an important digression on burgeoning corporate support for professorships and courses that teach the superiority of free enterprise.

II. Comparative Applications to MNCs

John Kenneth Galbraith has complained that the swelling plethora of literature on MNCs relates inversely to lucid diagnoses of their meaning.[16] In addition to my opening sketch on the significance of MNCs, I shall endeavor to identify and interrelate four aspects of MNCs: 1) their definitions and structures and 2) their adverse and humanizing consequences, real and potential. Then I can conclude with 3) a few samples of structural recommendations involving implicit moral maxims and 4) instances of regulatory guides, whether voluntarily or legally imposed by national and international agencies.

1. *Definitions and structures.* What is a multinational corporation? The variety of reported definitions stems not only from contrasting world views of those doing the defining (say from managerial windows or impoverished peoples' vistas). The multiple definitions also reflect the qualities and sizes of multinational structures. Among most common definitions is Arvind Phatoak's: MNCs are "interlocking networks of [autonomous, totally owned] subsidiaries [or else jointly owned affiliates] in several countries whose [managing] executives view the whole world as their theater."[17]

The definitional complexities related to MNCs are caused by forces promoting their vertical decentralization—like lingering nationalism or national coalitions like OPEC and the Andean Pact—and by forces that facilitate further vertical centralization, like the explosion of computer technology. Emphasis on vertical structures exists not only in socialist nation-state economies that, by the way, relate capitalistically to other nations. Attachment to the vertical also stands out in relatively single product economic units like the Ford Motor Company. Vertical organization is a pyramid where top management has freed itself from all but token interferences of owners or shareholders or at least from many of them. Management is the pharaoh who directs workers comprehending little of the total operation. The managerial pharaoh at the top of the pyramid coordinates the utilization of raw resources or basic skills, cuts down on global transportation costs, and further integrates production, distribution, and promotion without dependence on outside agencies. In the interest of efficiency workers and personnel understand little about the meaning of their contribution even though it may constitute their life's work.

A second kind of structure combines the advantages of vertical centralization with horizontal decentralization in dialectical interaction. A micro-image for these mergers or conglomerates or related products might be envisioned as a scene of family members, each of whom cooperatively agrees to give the grandparents separate but related presents needed for their anniversary voyage.

A third model on the spectrum of corporate structures is projected in systems of partly related and partly unrelated product divisions dealing with industrialization, utilities like A.T. & T., or financial services like Bankamerica Corporation. The concrete paradigm here is the fleet of ships or planes, monitored from abroad, each with its own independent captain left free to adapt to particular situations.[18]

In other words, the skeletal framework of MNC power varies from strict managerial control to the opposite pole of relatively detached financial or so-called portfolio pressures. The current trend toward more MNCs splintered into the fleet model means that cosmopolitan product or service divisions are now perceived to extend obvious advantages like the dynamics of speed, mobility, security, and versatile adaptability as opposed to more dysfunctional classical corporate structures. Yet, in every mixture along the spectrum there is found, for whatever motive, cooperation—like joint purchasing, research and development, and the ongoing game plans of avoiding double national taxations.[19]

On whatever logical bases the species of multinational enterprises are divided, the first concern among rich and poor alike is caused by the titanic size and strength, and the apparent inevitability of MNCs. As Galbraith admits, the question is no longer *whether* the MNC, but *whither?* Or how far?[20] The foregoing, oversimplified analysis is intended to help the reader to recognize the fascinating complexity, mobility, and consequent strategic strength of the various businesses called MNCs. But the overall issue of power should be dealt with more directly. This is so whether Christian or other traditions enjoin their adherents to stand against the principalities of this world or to risk direct, constructive involvement with Caesar's due. The risk involves the loss of innocent self-righteousness.

2. *The consequences of MNCs, beneficent and problematic.* Lesser developed countries (LDCs) that host MNCs tend to eye their mushrooming if not epidemic growth with primal awe and chronic suspicion. Their reaction occurs not only because sometimes the absentee parent management of MNCs is based in foreign nation-states. It also results because MNCs seem to represent the presence of a transnational, independent force that continues to outflank national laws and coalition agreements. Fear abides even when an MNC is parented from a single nation. It is felt that electronic transfer of funds, prices, and accounting systems can, with the aid of adept corporate lawyers, interact more swiftly, buoyantly, and innovatively than extant, stolid, national democratic or bureaucratic regulatory procedures. When the latter attempt to handle matters like disclosure of monopolistic wealth, taxes, employment practices, and so on, their speed and adaptability is less than breathtaking.

In sum, LDCs tend to picture MNCs not as the phoenix but as the modern dinosaur, to borrow Edwin P. Rome's symbols.[21] For some LDCs the MNC succeeds nation-states in their inequitable use of power and the inescapable wars that such abuse generates. At the opposite pole, others feel that since political structures like nation-states are helpless guardians of peace, therefore the survival and cooperation of human beings depends on economic structures like MNCs. MNCs are conceived as the successors to obsolescent political structures. In this conception schools of business are no longer training centers for a trade or an economically related profession. They are virtually schools of philosophy and statecraft. Their students will possess the platforms once held by philosophers and politicians. The following paragraphs attempt to delineate the grounds for these pessimistic and optimistic views, in reverse order.

Beneficent functions. Contrary to some of the understandable anxieties of third-world nations—or fourth-world nations redlined out of international trade because of their poverty—the historical cascade of MNCs since World War II has been associated with objectives more comprehensive than the MNCs' insular profits and their other problematic ends and results.

Optimistic prognoses for national and international benefits have been offered by known economists like the Keynesian Paul Samuelson,[22] Neil Jacoby,[23] or even Milton Friedman.[24] Their optimism varies to the degree that separate governments or national coalitions comply with their mixed Keynesian or more classical blueprints about governmental noninterference. Small attention, by the way, is placed upon the considerable governmental intervention that already subsidizes big business by way of tax incentives, tariffs on imports, or federal endowment for research and development, etc. Friedman himself, nevertheless, admits corporate hypocrisy about the acceptance of governmental aid for corporations while opposing it for others. "When U.S. Steel takes out full page ads to advertise the virtues of free enterprise, and then pleads to restrict imports on steel from Japan, people say, What a bunch of hypocrites! And they're right!" [25]

In any case, economists like those just mentioned foresee the development of MNCs on an international scope as the most reasonable trajectory leading toward a federation of world governments and cross-cultural pluralism. MNCs are further envisaged as the most efficient and adaptable planetary means for the exchange and distribution of food, other products, technology, managerial planning skills, employment, services, wealth, and therefore world peace.

The last critical achievement would make possible a comprehensive substitution of peaceful technologies for inflationary military expenditures that are devastating global resources and economies. In these variously hopeful purviews, corporate tax incentives would continue and technical loopholes would remain respected legal apertures—at least to the degree that no more than the present 50 percent taxation on U.S. MNCs should be effectively enforced. With benevolent regulations and incentives bolstered by national treaties and international agencies, wealth will presumably multiply for the greatest utility and good of the greatest number. This abundance may be supplemented by joint resolutions resulting from solemn reflections about the planet's depleting resources and failing, wounded ecosphere.

Problematic dysfunctions. When the focus is adjusted from long-range international scope to more immediate and local consequences for relatively destitute regions, the voices of the poor and the oppressed seem to drown out those who downplay the dysfunctions of MNCs for their benefits. To name a few problems plaguing host nations, especially host LDCs, the following may be isolated for special analysis.

First, drastic *unemployment and inflation* accompany capital investment and the parallel technological displacement of labor-intensive industry. Put more simply, MNC automation reduces jobs for both the skilled and the unskilled and peoples are polarized economically and politically. The phenomenon of MNC-related unemployment indicates that LDCs will continue attempting to contract eventual or partial ownership and management. Otherwise they may react by expropriation, noncooperation, or by pressuring entrenched MNCs to leave their countries. In 1978 the Indian Prime Minister Desai gambled on policies that would place a maximal number of Indians into the work force at the cost of losing the benefits that might have accrued from the ongoing presence of departing MNCs. Developments like MNC-occasioned unemployment imply that affirmative-action quotas may increasingly constitute a global issue with negative feedback from national labor unions of more affluent countries.

Second, in respect to *profits,* populations, and working personnel LDCs wonder why so much wealth is drained from their foundering economies. To them 50 percent taxation of the world's third largest pool of profits (based on U.S. industrial MNCs alone) seems far from exorbitant. At the same time they may well realize that no corporation is going to operate for gains less than they can make by indirect investments. However, if MNCs are to remain in LDCs as welcome guests, they will have to create new ways to invest in labor-intensive technologies in which local populations can be educated. Such is the middle maxim that justice seems to require.

Third, LDCs anguish about deepening ripples in their environmental pollution, depleting resources, and political stability. Fourth, and no less critically, LDCs are preoccupied not merely with belated romances with nationalism, but with a loss of national autonomy and cultural identity at several strata. These include religious, esthetic, psychological, and moral levels among others. Some citizens of LDCs dread dehumanizing materialism, the aimless absolutizing of consumption and of MNC growth for growth's sake, solely as an end. They also mourn the colossal billion-dollar briberies and cover-ups grudgingly admitted by some four hundred corporations in 1977 for the preceding six years.[26] Fifth, LDCs, like other countries, ponder the monopolistic effects of MNCs on the free enterprise of smaller businesses. This is a capitalistic mutation that transfigures capitalism as it was originally conceived. Lastly, from the viewpoint of parent nations, not all are convinced that their dwindling balances of payments are unrelated to MNC exportation of capital, jobs, and technological skills. They fear instead that their shrinking economies lead to national and global instability, both politically and militarily.[27] Concerned groups in all nations are afraid that these instabilities, combined with the ridiculous expansion of arms trade by aerospace industries like Lockheed and Northrop, can lead to the unthinkable.

3. *Structural and moral recommendations.* Not all quandaries and their resolutions are directly moral, but many are primarily structural. This lesson can be gleaned from modern MNCs themselves. Within the present limited frame of reference only a few structural, indirectly moral middle axioms can be advocated for further reflection on more particular maxims and case studies.

First, as it was briefly indicated above, Christian and other expressions of social justice require MNC disclosure or public "social audits." These should divulge and account for all the problematic factors mentioned previously: items like training indigenous personnel, joint sharing of ownership, management, and profits, standardized and intelligible accounts of cash flows, assets, debentures, and employment practices and benefits. Social audits should also review patent rights, trademarks, conflicts of interest, potential payoffs, and the final distribution figures about profits that actually reach the poor as well as the affluent. Host nations should define clearly and publicly their expectations and the public activities permissible to MNC personnel. In sum, value judgments and norms on disclosure and other rules (like education for employment) should consider social impacts at several points. These include technological exchange, ecology, politics, social and psychological alienation, and the cultural gamut of religious, ethical, esthetical, and other developments.[28] Coordinate measures must be taken to protect audited corporations from abuses of those disclosures by predatory competitors or other myopic interest groups. Perhaps the greatest challenge to the human imagination facing social audits is the simplification of the audit. At present, audits consume the bulk of the energies of top corporate leadership. Teachers and researchers face comparable difficulties. They waste several weeks each year drawing up reports on individual activities, committee actions, and research rationales that might attract support from grant agencies. The abuse of audits and individual accountability affects MNCs, smaller corporations, colleges and religious groups in public service. While some corporate lawyers despair that audits can ever function honestly, nondestructively, and efficiently, the reader may have more faith in the human imagination.

Public advocacy by corporations and interest groups. A second set of normative recommendations concerns not the audit but advocacy. At the level of advocacy by corporations and interest groups regulatory maxims may be tried experimentally or in more permanent forms, nationally or internationally, and with effective enforcements through voluntary agreement or law. Nowadays, interest groups embrace unconscionable organized terrorists whose aim is to subvert or unduly influence nations. They also include professional currency speculators and militant organizations that support causes no longer clearly identifiable as conservative, liberal or humanizing.

As for corporate advocacy, in the United States corporations like Citicorp[29] or representatives of the mass media may now legally buy or consume media time and space. The new goal is not merely to inform about or advertise their products, but to advocate stands on issues and on conflicts of interests, e.g., those relating to tax structures, gun controls, or the arms trade. In the defense of human beings who are preoccupied or easily misled and acquiescing, it seems that hortatory regulations should evolve swiftly into at least experimental legislation. Such rules would also protect credulous adults and children, those who are incapable of resisting thought paralysis by data gluts, and those unable to distinguish propaganda from persuasion.

4. *Regulatory agencies and group action, including religious group action.* This concluding section will adumbrate only four of the manifold and overlapping agencies that seek to implement, augment, or attenuate middle and proximate norms like those sketched above. In the name of cultural autonomy and pluralism, I shall preface this arbitrary selection with the middle maxim that no agency should require MNCs to shoulder the full responsibility for public needs and cultural developments. This axiom is derived from the goal of restraining MNC control over all aspects of human life. It also protects the immediate financial welfare of MNCs. The same counsel may be predicated for the regulatory responsibilities of any proposed agencies. The many centers of power—governmental, religious, legal, corporate, international, etc.—should remain decentralized, however much they aspire to avoid waste and duplication of effort. Unshared power will corrupt as inanely and indomitably as bureaucratic bungling. Further reference to governmental, trade, academic, and religious organizations and agencies will be reserved for note 30. But it should be noted that, in theory, any one of them might develop more fruitfully than the others.[30]

The four agencies to which I shall allude protect unions, management, and the public in general. 1. The International Labor Office (ILO) strives to consolidate concerted efforts by national unions which stand impervious to the fact that in the face of MNCs, union internationalization is less a danger for unions than it is their last best hope.[31] 2. The General Agreement on Tariffs and Trades (GATT): for better business and production this organization *exhorts* nations to levy indirect taxes on products only in the country of destination. 3. The United Nations' Conference on Trade and Development UNCTAD) among transnational corporations, together with a related UN center on MNCs, is viewed as ignominious by the editors of *Barron's* magazine on the grounds that it would legislate excessive disclosures. *Barron's* also fears redistribution of MNC funds to the poor that would affect Western based MNCs unfairly.[32] 4. Doubtless, some business sectors would prefer that a fourth and last organization should be further implemented: a *voluntary* business Organization for Economic Cooperation and Development (OECD). This agency would control bribery and other corrupt practices in which MNCs are both victims and partners in crime.

In concluding, I would like to stimulate the reader's further meditation on the need for comparative ethics and its application to MNCs. My objective has been to evoke curiosity rather than to help the reader to memorize lists of data or analytical observations. For those who would pursue the latter goal I have assembled in the notes a considerable list of resources in which the neglected subject of comparative business ethics may be further examined. I also wish to invite specific further reflection on the MNCs' involvement in armament industries.[33] Neil Jacoby has identified the 100 largest U.S. industrials as the 100 chief contractors for the U.S. Department of Defense, at least generally speaking. Howard H. Frederick adds that 20 percent of United States citizens earn their living from the arms industries, led by Northrop and Lockheed. He does not supply comparable figures to unveil the link between the sale of arms and the economy of the emerging superpower, Brazil, or of other countries that specialize in arms production. But he does add very specific proposals as to how the skills of armament workers could be transferred to peaceful technology and services. Otherwise, the potential consequences are ominous. While the U.S. and the U.S.S.R. purchase 60 percent of these armaments from industries like those just mentioned, Middle Eastern trade has quadrupled since 1965.

Although the arms trade is not strictly an MNC dilemma, still it symbolizes the gravity of the problems and regulations for MNCs under discussion. It also underscores the contemporary assessment that ethics must proceed with cross-cultural sensitivity, a non-provincial ethos, and comparative criteria. In this spirit, ethics needs above all to particularize middle maxims concerning the key economic infrastructures of humanity's common future.

In my judgment, it is not compatible with Christian and other religio-moral traditions that their adherents should merely sit on the sidelines and prophetically criticize the imaginative efforts of others. Religious and other humanists must risk involvement in proposing international regulations for professionals to clarify, legislate, and implement. They may also pressure for them in interest groups or lobby for them politically. As long as symbols like the original garden, stewardship, incarnation or divine presence, and resurrection or divine promise are not proved to be counterfeit, Christian and other traditional responsibilities for the future of MNCs are clear.

Just as the structures and consequences of MNCs affect people individually and socially, they can respond in the same two dimensions. As individuals they can become more conscious of the significance and strategies of MNCs. In the performance of this task they might utilize such tools as the *Directory of Corporate Affiliates* or *Dun and Bradstreet's Million Dollar Directory* to ascertain who owns whom, what decisions affect their immediate environment, personal lives and concerns, and who makes the decisions. When individual consciousness is raised, the routes to civil or religious centers for study and action become more obvious.

The possibilities for moral response surpass use of the media, demonstrations, or political lobbying and campaigning. Imposing, if not stunning, new potential can be glimpsed in the fact that by 1985 the pension funds of U.S. workers alone will exceed 1 trillion dollars and "are expected to provide almost one-half of all the external capital raised by U.S. corporations in the next decade."[34] If pensioners take their due control from present money managers, they can decide where, how, and for what ends their capital should be invested. "Everyman" might control MNCs after all—for better or for worse.

Social and nonmyopic interest groups are the call of the hour. Gradually, with the lessons learned from trial and error, professional results might occur. Entombed ideals might stir alive in the dawn of moral action.

Notes

1. *Sources: U.N. Transnational Corporations in World Development: A Reexamination* (New York: 1978), pp. 280–312. See table IV.1 for lists and statistical comparisons of the top 500 U.S. and foreign-based MNCs.

2. *Sources,* pp. 216–18; tables 111–13: world's fifty largest banks ranked by size of total assets at the end of 1976; table III–14: thirteen largest U.S.-based transnational bank foreign earnings, 1970–1975.

3. See *ibid.* for thorough statistical analyses of U.S. and foreign-based MNCs. See also *Fortune* (May 8, 1976), 240ff. on the 500 largest industrial corporations, most of which are MNCs. The most startling profile apparent within the top 20 industrials is that except for IBM, GE, and IT&T the top 13 are either oil or automobile corporations. By my computation annual sales in 1977 for 10 of the top 13 corporations (oil and automobile) reached over 286 billion dollars, or over a quarter of the gross national product. Abstracting from numerous related industries, it seems clear that the present U.S. economy depends essentially on the automobile industry. At present I leave the manifold implications about waste relative to other world needs to the imagination of the reader.

4. See Nasrollah S. Fatemi and Gail W. Williams, *Multinational Corporations* (Cranbury, New Jersey: A.S. Barnes and Co., Inc., 1975) p. 210. On p. 219 the authors summarize data from U.N. studies to underline 1) the MNC presence in petroleum, computers, banking, and the hotel and recreation industries, and 2) the importance of MNCs in interlocking the economies and peaceful common interests of most developed countries. The contribution to global peace and survival is as impressive as the proliferation of arms industries is threatening. Further information on intertwining economies can be found in Juvenal L. Angel, *Directory of American Firms Operating in Foreign Countries* (8th ed.; New York: Simon and Schuster, Inc., 1975).

5. See Roderick Hindery, *Comparative Ethics in Hindu and Buddhist Traditions* (Delhi: Motilal Banarsidass, 1978), 307 pp., including an introductory chapter on comparative method in general, sections and charts on comparative conclusions, and comprehensive lists of Asian primary and secondary source materials. See also Hindery, "Catholicity of Ethical Sources: Neglected Key to Christian Unity," *Journal of Ecumenical Studies (JES)* 15/4 (Fall 1978); "Ethics and Esthetics in Asian Traditions: Confucianism, A Paradigm for Western Religions and Social Change," *JES* 15/2 (Spring 1978), 227–42; "Exploring Comparative Ethics," *JES* 10/3 (Summer 1973), 552–74; "Muslim and Christian Ethics," *Cross Currents* 22/4 (Winter 1973), 381–97; "Pluralism in Moral Theology: Reconstructing Ethical Pluralism," *CTSA Proceedings 1973,* 71–94. Earlier trial versions of three of the book's ten chapters and two appendices were published and are also available as "Hindu Ethics in the *Rāmāyana,*" *The Journal of Religious Ethics* 4/2 (Fall 1976), 287–322; "Hindu Ethics as Reflected in Some Popu-

lar Indian Classics," *Insight: A Journal of World Religions* 2/1 (Spring 1977), 15–28: and "Windows in Interreligious Ethics: *The Bhagavadgītā,*" *"The Journal of Religious Studies* 6/1 (Spring 1978), 112–32. My initial insistence (*JES* 10/3) on the need for grounding normative ethics has been recently elaborated by John Reeder, "Religious Ethics as a Field and a Discipline," *Journal of Religious Ethics* 6 (Spring 1978), 46–48.

6. See Daniel Maguire, *The Moral Choice* (Garden City, New York: Doubleday and Co., Inc., 1978).

7. Often such syntheses result in the confirmation or launching of world views and anthropologies that tend to lock principled decisions into automatic pilot.

8. Typical of the perduring use of middle rules in case applications is David Hollenbach, "Modern Catholic Teachings Concerning Justice," in John C. Haughey, ed., *The Faith That Does Justice* (New York: Paulist Press, 1977), pp. 207–31. See also Charles E. Curran's *Ongoing Revision: Studies in Moral Theology* (Notre Dame: Fides, 1975). Richard McCormick's annual "Notes on Moral Theology," *Theological Studies* (e.g., 39/1 [March 1978] 88–116) offer evidence and summaries of the persistent, audacious focus of Catholic and other moralists on maxims and case studies. Previous legalistic, casuistical clubs had brought casuistry into early disrepute by quoting only themselves to the neglect of other sources and reflective analyses. Less narrow case studies have weathered the antinormative attacks of Marxists, moral relativists, ethical language analysts, and existentialists. An intriguing historical review of the development of moral maxims for economics can be located in Rudolf Skandera, *Canonist Ethics: Origin of Economic Thought and Management Practices* (Rio de Janeiro: Fundacão Getulio Vargas, 1972). John C. Bennett's analytical studies of middle maxims, e.g., in *Christian Ethics and Social Policy* (New York: Charles Scribner's Sons, 1946), pp. 77–83 are expanded in Philip Wogaman, *A Christian Method of Moral Judgment* and *The Great Economic Debate* (Philadelphia: The Westminster Press, 1976 and 1977). An introduction to parallel philosophical literature on teleological and deontological middle rules exists in Wm. Frankena, *Ethics* (2d ed.; Englewood Cliffs, New Jersey: Prentice-Hall, Inc., 1973), pp. 25–28, 39–42, and 55.

9. See Fatemi and Williams, *Multinational Corporations*, pp. 207–28 and Robert Emmett Tindall, *Multinational Enterprises* (Dobbs Ferry, N.Y.: Oceana Publications, 1975), pp. i-xv and 106–291.

10. For primary Confucian references see Hindery, "Ethics and Esthetics in Confucianism," 227, 231, and 238.

11. Detailed information on qualities attributed to the Japanese people is assembled in S. Prakash Sethi, *Japanese Business and Social Conflict: A Comparative Analysis of Response Patterns with American Business* (Cambridge, Mass.: Ballinger Publishing Co., 1975), pp. 38–47.

12. Richard H. Viola, *Organizations in Changing Society: Administration and Human Values* (Philadelphia: W.B. Saunders Co., 1977).

13. See the section on "Business Honesty" in Norman Lamm, *The Good Society: Jewish Ethics in Action* (New York: The Viking Press, 1974), pp. 149–54 and sections 1–4 on love and compassion.

14. E. F. Schumacher, *Small Is Beautiful: Economics as if People Mattered* (New York: Harper and Row, 1973), pp. 53–63 on "Buddhist Economics."

15. Donald G. Jones, *A Bibliography of Business Ethics, 1971–1975* (Charlottesville: University Press of Virginia, 1977).

16. "Who Controls MNCs?" *Harvard Business Review* 53 (November 1975), 97–100. In addition to Galbraith's widely acclaimed *The New Industrial State* and *The Age of Uncertainty* see his *Economics and the Public Purpose* (Boston: Houghton Mifflin Co., 1973).

17. Arvind Phatak, *Managing Multinational Corporations* (New York: Praeger Publishers, 1974), p. 21. See also Phatak, *Evolution of World Enterprises* (New York: American Management Association, 1971).

18. See *ibid.*, pp. 20, 72–85.

19. Fully technical analyses of MNCs utilize other bases of division, such as a) international, single parent MNCs, b) geographically separated MNCs whose subsidiaries or partial affiliates are divided by nation or region, c) worldwide product structures, and d) mixtures of all of these. See Phatak's exposition of divisions in his *Managing Multinational Corporations*, pp. 172–88; also Frederick D. Sturdivant, *Business and Society: A Managerial Approach* (Homewood, Illinois: Richard D. Irwin, Inc., 1977), pp. 414–43; and Frederick D. Sturdivant and Larry M. Robinson, *The Corporate Social Challenge: Cases and Commentaries* (Homewood, Illinois: Richard D. Irwin, Inc., 1977), pp. 277–346.

20. "Who Controls MNCs?" *passim.*

21. See Edwin P. Rome, "The Multinational Enterprise: Dinosaur or Phoenix?" in S. Prakash Sethi and Richard H. Holton, *Management of the Multinationals: Policies, Operations, and Research* (New York: The Free Press, 1974), pp. 77–87. Other materials relevant to the interactions between MNCs and LDCs exist in R. Hal Mason, "Conflicts Between Host Countries and the Multinational Enterprise," *California Management Review* (Fall 1974); related articles by M. P. Sloan, R. E. Muller, and Louis Turner in Robert L. Heilbroner and Paul London, eds., *Corporate Social Policy: Selections from Business and Society Review* (Reading, Mass.: Addison-Wesley Publishing Co., 1973); Abdul A. Said and Luiz R. Simmons, eds., *The New Sovereigns: Multinational Corporations as World Powers* (Englewood Cliffs, New Jersey: Prentice-Hall, Inc., 1971); Sanjaya Lall and Paul Streeten, *Foreign Investments, Transnationals and Developing Countries* (Oxford University Press, 1978); and Michael Akehurst, *A Modern Introduction to International Law* 3d ed.; New York: Allen and Unwin, 1977).

22. Paul Samuelson, *Economics* (10th ed.; New York: McGraw-Hill Book Co., 1974), pp. 680–82, 690–91.

23. Neil H. Jacoby, *Corporate Power and Social Responsibility* (New

York: Macmillan Publishing Co., Inc., 1973). See also George F. Rohrlich, *Social Economics: Concepts and Perspectives,* ed. by Barrie O. Pellman (Bradford, England: MCB Books, 1977).

24. Milton Friedman, *Freedom and Capitalism* (Chicago: University of Chicago Press, 1962). A thorough if partisan historical background for grasping the ideas of Friedman and other leading modern economists exists in Robert Lekachman's *A History of Economic Ideas* (New York: McGraw-Hill Book Co., 1959).

25. Quotation from James Daniel, "Milton Friedman: Capitalism's Champion," *The Reader's Digest* (June 1978), 156–59. The new legal phenomenon of issue advertising for principles of laissez-faire capitalism merits extensive discussion. I have estimated that twenty-five leading advertising agencies (twenty-one in the U.S., three in Japan and one in France) listed $12,913,000,000 in 1976 for total and foreign billings. If this kind of backing directs itself increasingly to issue advocacy, new problems will arise for interest groups who cannot afford equal time. See *Sources,* Table III-15. Such advocacy has now entered those citadels of freedom and nonpartisan views called colleges and universities. "The Goodyear Tire and Rubber Co., for instance, has given Kent State University $250,000 to set up the Goodyear Professorship of Free Enterprise" and "industry has already underwritten 100 courses intended to teach the superiority of free enterprise"—a practice approved by former Secretary of the U.S. Treasury, William E. Simon. Quotations from Fred M. Hechinger, "Currents: The Corporation in the Classroom," *Saturday Review* (September 16, 1978), 14–15. Hechinger also wonders if the acceptance of foreign endowments will, with parallel logic, require expressing the donors' points of view about issues like Iranian or Saudi Arabian oil production.

26. See Hans Schollhammer, "Ethics in an International Business Context," *California Management Review* 25/2 (Spring 1977), 53–63 and *The New York Times* (Dec. 21, 1976).

27. For contrasting findings confer *The U.S. Chamber of Commerce, United States Multinational Enterprise Survey* (1960–1970). pp. 25–30. Fatemi and Williams summarize it in *Multinational Corporations,* pp. 95–106.

28. See Keith Davis and Robert L. Blomstrom, *Business and Society: Environment and Responsibility* (New York: McGraw-Hill Book Co., 1975), esp. pp. 175, 503–17.

29. See the Citicorp ad in *Saturday Review* (September 16, 1978).

30. 1. *Governmental agencies* include the Andean Pact, OPEC, the U.S. Senate, Tariff Commission, Dept. of Commerce, FTC, FCC, and SEC. In 1978 the U.S. Comptroller of the Currency called for a separate supervisory unit for large multinational banks (*Wall Street Journal,* May 24, 1978). 2. *Trade groups* include Business for Public Action, the International Monetary Fund (IMF), International Chamber of Commerce Guidelines, International Bank for Reconstruction and Development (IBRD), and the 1972 regulations of the International Confederation of Free Trade Unions. 3.

Among *academic centers and agencies* are those at the University of Virginia, GTU, and various journals and schools of business. For a fuller listing of agencies see Phatak, *Managing Multinational Corporations,* pp. 49–55. *Religious groups* include the Interfaith Center for Corporate Responsibility, the Brazilian Episcopal Conference, etc. These agencies, the media, and interest groups share the primary task of identifying all constituencies affected by MNCs.

31. See Tindall, *Multinational Enterprises,* pp. 264–77.

32. *Barron's* (May 13, 1978), p. 7.

33. See Howard H. Frederick, *The Arms Trade and the Middle East: A Primer* (Philadelphia: American Friends Service, 1977).

34. Jeremy Rifkin and Randy Power, "Pension Power: Meet the New Masters of American Industry," *Saturday Review* (September 2, 1978), 11–15; adapted from their book *The North Will Rise Again: Politics and Power in the 1980s* (Boston: Beacon Press, 1978).

Theological Guidance for Moral Development Research

Paul J. Philibert

A great many persons consider Kohlberg's six stages of moral development as a ray of hope in an otherwise grim moral landscape. Kohlberg himself encourages such an attitude: "In days which at times seem like the decline of the American empire, in which there are so many examples of power corrupting, we need to look at universal foundations of integrity."[1] Another observer of our culture claims that "internalized values from an earlier period in our moral history no longer hold good."[2] So we end up looking and feeling to ourselves as dangerously amoral, and that impression is magnified by the dramatic quality and the increasing quantity of changes in our social and moral environment. Many educators have despaired of communicating traditional ideals.[3] Philip Rieff comments:

> Western men are sick precisely of those interior ideals which have shaped their characters. Accordingly, they feel they have no choice except to try to become free characters.
>
> What characterizes modernity, I think, is just this idea that men need not submit to any power—higher or lower—other than their own.[4]

Such observations may help to explain the very strong attraction that Kohlberg's "natural direction" in moral education exercises upon those who come to learn about it. According to Kohlberg, students can be taught to construct the moral universe they live in. What jogs students along on the path toward mature moral reasoning, Kohlberg optimistically believes, is mental conflict ("cognitive disequilibrium") aroused by some situation which doesn't make sense in terms of their existing set of moral categories. There is a promise, hidden beneath this formula, to produce citizens who are both self-directed and also fundamentally compatible with their fellows regarding their goal directions.

Kohlberg isn't shy about indicating his model for moral success. It is American "constitutional" morality. He believes that the United States is the first civilization built upon postconventional moral principles, that our Constitution is a stage five document, and that all the difficulties we've had and are having, from Watergate to My Lai to the generation gap, can be overcome by stage-development education. "The current concern for moral education," he says, represents an awareness of a demand for a higher or postconventional level of moral principles in our national life."[5] Some have commented upon the incongruity of a conventional order whose moral goal is postconventional citizens.[6] Perhaps a better way to make this point is to indicate that Kohlberg's notion of principled moral reasoning seems always to entail individualism and standing apart from the crowd because of one's principles. As Carl Bereiter keenly observes about Kohlberg's theory:

> there seems to be an explicit ideology that says damn convention, let everyone work out his or her own morality, and an implicit ideology that says that the majority shall define what is right.[7]

Such complaints notwithstanding, Kohlberg's aspirations for a society where people have a sense of direction again, a just society where citizens can establish justice within unforeseen new contexts of social interaction, is an attractive goal. No serious thinker is opposed, in principle at least, to such an aspiration for moral education.

Moral Education

As a phrase, "moral education" nowadays connotes two particular trends in pedagogy, both of which are psychologically conceptualized and both of which are developmental. Both of these trends represent metaphors for growth. Just as the human body grows in the process of incorporating and integrating nutrients, gradually differentiating the areas of development according to the total or organismic needs of the individual, so morality also grows. Within this developmental point of view, mature morality represents the elaboration of structures of adequacy intended by nature itself, while a fixation at lower or inadequate levels of thinking or behavior represents a case of obstacles or impediments to moral development.

One of these trends of moral education is Freudian. As Philip Rieff summarizes:

> The Freudian school [contends] that once certain primary patterns of emotional relation to the mother and father . . . are established, most people develop morally along a series of events that can be traced back to that very early set pattern. The pattern keeps repeating itself, even though the individual "growing up" in this pattern is rarely aware of the pattern, nor can he have any conscious memory of how it established itself.[8]

In this model, however successful later growth may be, the early emotional pattern of relational responses will control the direction of responses of the adult according to childhood experiences.

The most viable exponent of this theory, at least in terms of its impact upon moral education, is Erik Erikson. His "life cycle" of eight stages is fundamentally Freudian in its conception. While it is a helpful analytic and explanatory tool, it does not lend itself precisely to strategies for moral education in the same sense that Kohlberg's stages do. But Erikson's work is worth mentioning here, since it is developmental in conception and since its focus is upon moral development in its relation to affective development and the integration of experience with more adequate self-understanding.[9]

The other trend in moral education is Piagetian. Jean Piaget places much less emphasis than the Freudian school on repression, sexual development, and identity. Piaget's concern is cognitive, although for him and his followers cognition is not radically set apart from affect or from behavior. Piaget believes that "thinking" is for "doing": that thinking is itself an activity or operation. Consequently, Piaget's developmental stages are expressed in terms of the gradual build-up of resources for adult mental operations, the construction of logic and empathic perspective-taking. Piaget calls the condition where a child is bound to "a certain narrow-minded self-reference"[10] the period of *heteronomy*. A later period, which generally develops as the child's logical capacities develop, sees the reasons for the way society fits together and is called *autonomy*.

Kohlberg became fascinated with this contribution of two stages of moral reasoning that he got from Piaget. Kohlberg set about trying to establish greater detail in describing the movement from heteronomy to autonomy and in the further elaboration of post-adolescent autonomy. From his early work interviewing teen-age boys, he arrived at six stages of moral development, based on Piaget's foundational intuitions, which run from young childhood to late maturity.[11]

Kohlberg tells, in *Readings in Moral Education,* about how his then graduate student and later colleague Moshe Blatt initiated the strategy that has become Kohlberg's moral education program.[12] Since moral subjects only understand stages that are no more than one beyond their own, and since the same subjects are nonetheless attracted to reasoning in that stage just one beyond their dominant stage, Blatt devised classroom interventions to provide discussion and reasoning that would expose students to such higher-stage thinking. And thus was born the moral development intervention strategy.

Through schoolroom activities and adult education programs, many Americans have heard about Kohlberg's strategies for moral education. Most people casually acquainted with this material have heard of Kohlberg's claims to have found universally valid moral stages. However fewer are aware that Kohlberg's moral education intervention, while it proposes to stimulate advanced moral reasoning, does not claim to lead to right answers or solved problems. The most that a moral education strategy can hope to accomplish, on the basis of language cues—e.g., "getting in trouble" for stage one, "looking good" for stage three, "doing your duty" for stage four, etc.—is to identify higher-stage thinking. An accompanying confidence that higher-stage thinking will more likely produce better solutions to moral problems than would lower-stage thinking is an unproven commitment (which I, by the way, find congenial as a general assumption).

It strikes me as significant, then, to place the valuable, if limited, contributions of Kohlberg's research and theory in the context of Christian moral education. De facto, many religious educators are using Kohlberg's stages in their teaching. It has to be made clear for them that this stage theory is an insufficient resource for Christian conscience formation. Further, I want to suggest to others who are doing creative work in the area of moral education that some guidance for their research is available from reflection upon the theological commitments that we share in the Christian faith tradition.

Theological Guidance for Moral Education

A variety of complaints have been made already about the un-congenial nature of Kohlberg's theoretical apparatus as a resource for Christian moral education or moral catechesis.[13] Crittenden emphasizes that Kohlberg's position commits his followers to a particular interpretation of morality and to certain moral beliefs in preference to others. For example, Kohlberg's ethical groundwork

> restricts morality to the range of concepts (such as rights, obligation, duty) associated with justice . . .
> It involves the rejection of various positions that make some claim to be moral as, for example, moral conventionalism, religiously based morality . . .
> [It likewise rejects] any position that appeals to absolute moral standards (the view that there are certain actions one is never justified in doing regardless of the consequences).[14]

Others have criticized Kohlberg's position for dismissing the classic Western philosophy of virtue with irrelevant argumentation and thereby diminishing the meaning of moral education as a result of this arbitrary limitation of the scope of moral reflection.[15] Thus, Kohlberg's work as it stands is problematic for those who would use it in religious education, since it takes neither religious allegiance, virtue, nor moral absolutes seriously.

These comments, however, are merely context for the work at hand. Kohlberg has chosen the route he will follow and seems determined to stick to it, despite criticism that goes well beyond the preoccupations mentioned here.[16] Rather than focus upon these limitations, I would like to shift the focus to other items that are also of interest to anyone exploring the gradual maturation of the psychology of moral development as an area of study, and of special interest to religious educators who are looking for guidance in their own domain.

My thesis here is as follows: certain doctrines of Christian faith can offer to the believer insight and direction about the maturation of adult morality. Many critics observe that Kohlberg is on thinner ice in describing his postconventional stages than he is in his descriptions of stages one through four.[17] Consequently, the interpretation of postconventional reasoning (stages five and six) will be more convincing if it can be shown to be compatible with the theological vision of Christian faith. Some of the agenda for moral education research can be and should be taken from the indications that doctrinal explorations may offer about the development of the mature Christian person.

The three areas of Christian doctrine I have chosen to explore are: (1) the doctrine of creation and its implications for human relatedness; (2) the doctrine of the Holy Spirit and its implications for a kind of adult heteronomy; and (3) the doctrine of the Cross and the moral value of suffering.

(1) A Dynamic Understanding of Creaturely Relatedness

Acknowledging God as my Creator means not only that I imaginatively construct some moment in the past in which God intervened to establish my existence. Being my Creator includes even now being the present source from which my existence—which is metaphysically a gift—continually flows.

Why is this important? I think it is essential in order to avoid a kind of rationalism which would suggest that my *relatedness* to God is consequent upon my understanding of and upon my assent to the idea of such a relation. The point is subtle, but it has implications of some consequence.

Observe Kohlberg's reflections in this area:

Psychologically I believe that it takes a long time to work out a moral stage in terms of its elaboration as an organized pattern of belief and feeling about the cosmos which Fowler calls a faith stage. Philosophically I incline to Kant's solution, that faith is grounded on moral reason because moral reason "requires" faith rather than that moral reason is grounded on faith.[18]

Kohlberg's phrase, "moral reason 'requires' faith rather than that moral reason is grounded on faith," articulates his position vis-à-vis certain fundamentals of moral-development and faith-development theory. It means that "faith" as understood by Kohlberg is: (a) homogeneous with moral development in terms of its mode of development, (b) a phenomenon that comes as a fruition of the long struggle of stage development, and (c) a kind of reasonable postulate at which one arrives in the light of more mature moral sentiment (moral reason "requires" faith).

An everyday illustration of the consequences of such an attitude may be the issue of the meaningfulness of ritual worship in church. Parents and religious educators have heard adolescents insist that they really don't have any reason to go to church, since Sunday worship "doesn't mean anything to me" or "isn't relevant to me." Such an attitude presupposes that worship is not meaningful until I personally discover the moral or religious emotions which would convey that meaning. The moral and religious subjectivism that underlies this attitude is not likely to lead at any point to a persuasion of the rightness of worship without some objective orientation to the inescapable reality of being related to the Creator whom one adores and thanks in religious ritual.

This does not mean that someone can be coerced into healthy religion "in spirit and in truth." But I do suggest that an appreciation for worship proceeds from other sources than merely rational investigation, even of one's own self and feelings. As with so many other areas of our cultural heritage that take on substantial meaning in adulthood, religion also begins largely with imitation, with learning by doing. A purely rational quest for religion or for faith is not going to find much to identify as significant in the earliest stages of personal development.

It is interesting to observe that religion as conceived by Thomas Aquinas in his Summa Theologiae was an objective orientation of moral principle within his theological synthesis, closely related to the doctrine of the creation. Aquinas's theory, which is representative of a point of view that was maintained in Roman Catholicism for many centuries, envisaged religion as the disposition and the act of believers who thereby acknowledged their indebtedness for the totality of their being to the Creator who begets them. Aquinas placed this thesis under his consideration of the virtue of justice—which deals with giving to others what is their due.

Since his notion of creation is not that of a one-time intervention, but rather that of a continual loving largesse (conservatio in esse: holding the creature in existence, is his term),[19] the connotations of the category of justice are not cold and impersonal. The "debt" of the creature to the Creator is not that of a juridical procedure in a court of law, but rather possesses the same quality as the divine initiative, namely, a loving relationship that acknowledges the spontaneous and free benevolence that sustains the gift of creaturely existence.[20]

In the Kohlberg paper referred to above, a loving "faith" appears to be a postconventional phenomenon in his theory. Preconventional and conventional faith are submerged into their deference to imposing authorities and legalism. Only at stage five does "divinity ... become identified with ... the ground of inner free-dom, individuality and responsibility."[21] This question of conceiv-ing fundamental religious experiences—be it faith or be it religious conscience—as postconventional phenomena needs to be addressed. I have already dealt with this question with respect to "con-science."[22] Christian faith posits the creature's relatedness to the Creator as primordial—preexisting either my *capacity* or my *will-ingness* to acknowledge the relation. What I called in the paper just cited "originary consciousness"—the dim and timid awareness of creatureliness and of the benevolence of the Creator—is central both to faith and to conscience. Moreover, this radical phenomenon of moral and religious experience is not postconventional in any stage theory, but a dimension of experience that is itself develop-mental and tolerant of stage description in its own right.

The point of these observations, it should be clear, is not to fault Kohlberg for failing to acknowledge doctrines of the Christian faith. He has no commitment to do so. But it should be obvious that a Christian creedal commitment to the doctrine of creation as a perduring benevolent love may find Kohlberg's description of "faith" and his theoretical attitude about the direction of theologi-cal experience (moral reason "requires" [i.e., arrives rationally at seeing the need for] faith) uncongenial. The Christian doctrine of the creation would require something like the following parameters for moral development and faith-development theory:

Developmental stages would understand the creature as primordially established in a relationship of benevolent love with the Creator (a relationship that has conse-quences for horizontal relationships with others who share that same creaturely dependence).

Religion/faith/religious conscience is a dimension that has its own developmental story, realized in one way in childhood experience and in other ways in more adult phases.

Religion/faith/religious conscience represents the awareness and response of the creature to a divine goodness disclosed in hidden and elusive ways and cannot be con-fused with either intuitive adult altruism or with occasion-al religious emotions that are essentially aesthetic in character.

(2) The Doctrine of the Spirit

Moral-development theory (and Fowler's faith-development

theory as well) has followed the general pattern established by Piaget in his *The Moral Judgment of the Child*. Piaget divided the child's moral judgments into two broad categories of the *heteronomous* and the *autonomous*. At the stage of heteronomy, young children perceive rules as external laws that are sacred and inflexible, arbitrary and beyond their capacity to comprehend fully. As children develop more and more understanding of why things are the way they are, they acquire the stage of autonomy. In the autonomous stage children can see the relationship between the rule and its outcome, they can understand the reason for there being such a law, and they are able to assent to legal expectations as reasonable demands. This is as far as Piaget takes the matter.

Kohlberg sought to "fill in" the gaps, by making the stages in the development from heteronomy to autonomy more precise as well as by carrying the development of Piaget's autonomous stage as far as he could into adult development. In doing so, Kohlberg asserted that the end point of moral development is a refined autonomy:

> I believe then, like Kant, that ultimate moral principles, Stage 6 morality, can and should be formulated and justified on grounds of autonomous moral rationality.[23]

The "autonomous moral rationality" mentioned here, moreover, is concerned exclusively with resolving conflicting claims of justice. As Kohlberg insists elsewhere:

> We make no direct claims about the ultimate aims of men, about the good life, or about other problems which a teleological theory must handle. These are problems beyond the scope of the sphere of morality or moral principles, which we define as principles of choice for resolving conflicts of obligation.[24]

Two observations of consequence need to be established here. The first is that Kohlbergian moral theory envisages the developmental sequence as a uniform movement of a subject from heteronomy to autonomy. The tonality of the heteronomy changes: from the incompetence of the unsocialized child fearing bad consequences whenever things are not clear to him, through the defensiveness of the early institutionalized child seeking constant reas-

surance through approval, into the gradual dissolution of heteronomy with the acquisition of custodial attitudes toward society in
stage four. Finally, once autonomy is established, Kohlberg's postconventional stages celebrate moral maturity as progressive individualism achieving a critical posture before the social contract.[25]
Autonomy for Kohlberg demands ever more transparent understanding of the order of things—the dissolution of mystery and the
increasing clarity of the rational imperative. In true idealist fashion, Kohlberg says: "Impersonality, ideality, universalizability,
preemptiveness, etc., are the formal characteristics of a moral judgment."[26]

Having thus examined some of the characteristics of Kohlbergian moral stage theory, I want to point out that a Christian theological context would make creedal demands somewhat at odds with
these ideas. The doctrine of the Holy Spirit's teaching within the
prayerful discernment of the believer calls for a growing sensitivity
to the mysterious, elusive, yet ever more demanding movement of
the Spirit of God. Christ promised the gift of the Holy Spirit to
those who believed in him; Paul taught that the faithful are moved
by the Spirit and "that the whole redeemed community is constituted by the Holy Spirit as its principle of life" and that this "is manifest in their behavior."[27]

Rejoining the question of autonomy, this doctrine of the Holy
Spirit seems to demand a vision of moral development that reaches
not only from heteronomy to autonomy, but one that moves from
an inframoral heteronomy through a moral autonomy and into a
supramoral heteronomy. Only in such a way can one explain the reality of pneumatology, the doctrine of the Holy Spirit, in the Christian life.

This kind of understanding of autonomy and responsibility
seems to be what Louis Monden had in mind in *Sin, Liberty and
Law*. There he wrote as follows:

> Whereas the outer pressure of taboo upon instinct entailed
> an inframoral heteronomy of the law, the heteronomy of
> the divine invitation to love is the basis of a supramoral
> ethics.[28]

In the light of my earlier insistence that *religion/faith* needs to be
seen as a distinct dimension whose presence is assured in moral-development theory from the earliest stages, something needs to be

said about how the doctrine of the Holy Spirit implies a heteronomy→autonomy→heteronomy pattern for an understanding of the overall development of moral sensibilities in the Christian.

As a developmental dimension, *religion/faith* develops according to its own patterns.[29] If this religious development were a discrete phenomenon, like the acquisition of a set of physical skills, then perhaps there would be no need to insist upon a supramoral heteronomy. But the realities of this religious dimension of human experience gradually establish a primacy in the Christian life (according to its New Testament description). Therefore, in the later stages of the Christian life, prayerful discernment, the gifts of the Holy Spirit, and a growing concrete sense of the presence of God have an impact upon the purely rational estimation of what is moral in any situation. Thus, though *religion/faith* represents a developmental dimension on its own, this dimension at its maturity interrelates with and governs the moral sensibilities of the Christian believer.

While this aspect of moral development needs to be "spelled out" through research and empirical investigation, it is more than a hypothesis. It is a position guided by the implications of the Christian doctrine of the Holy Spirit.

(3) The Doctrine of the Paschal Mystery—the Folly of the Cross

At times, moral development theory can sound like a kind of liberal utopianism. While Kohlberg claims that his stages are not indoctrination because they merely facilitate stage movement toward a natural goal of human development, some critics see his stages as pleading for a liberal, competitive political philosophy.[30] For some, the sequential, hierarchical, progressive qualities of his theory come across as too cheerful and optimistic to fit reality. Granted, the theory (in Kohlberg's hands a least) is not a theory of personality, but a theory of moral stages. Yet it seems, despite some efforts on Kohlberg's part to disclaim such an intention, unrealistically optimistic. Its rationalism seems to have no way to speak positively of pain, failure, frustration, waiting and tragedy.

Granting the usefulness of moral stages as an analytical tool, one must still speak firmly of the necessity for a broader appreciation of moral force than what the stages portray. A good deal of life falls through the sieve of the six stages. Much of human experience simply cannot be described as moral striving toward the affirmation of obligatory or adequate goals. Much of moral experience can only be described as a resistance to destructiveness, a *negation of negativities.* Quite often, the essential moral challenge of a moment of growth will not be precisely in the discernment of the right goal or means, but simply in the ability to go on, to keep moving, to try again—in the face of obstacles and absurdities. In other words, courage and hope are necessary to complete the Christian picture of moral development.

The inability to find any substantive moral significance in hope or perseverance demonstrates that Kohlberg's ethical rationalism ultimately has no portal into transcendence. While Kohlberg will avow that his stage six person should be endowed with qualities like selflessness or compassion, he has yet to demonstrate how such desirable qualities can derive from the "autonomous moral rationality" that is the substance of his ideal of mature moral experience.

In contrast to this, the central theological proclamation of the New Testament is God's acceptance of us when we were unacceptable. The Gospel proclaims divine mercy and forgiveness. The cross of Jesus is the symbol of the divine initiative. The irony of a divine predilection for those unlikely ever to be virtuoso exponents of "autonomous moral rationality" is a precious donation of Christian doctrine to moral theory. The forgiveness of the Gospel is not the reluctant readmission of those who fail back into the arena of rule-playing. New Testament forgiveness is a world view that insists upon the untidy freedom of God to sustain defenseless creatures with his love, to purify the singlemindedness of believers with trials of every sort, and to insist upon the utter gratuity of his gifts.

This New Testament theology, however, as much as it may oppose our conventional attitudes, comes across as less like a fairy tale than does an Apollonian theory of moral rationalism. Monden evokes the realism necessary as a context for any serious discussion of human freedom and stage development:

> The average individual, even if not neurotic, lives continually under the influence of *neuroticizing factors.* He has to live with a host of unassimilated deformations, tyrannical automatisms, paralyzing anxieties, obsessive impulses or hungry frustrations . . .
>
> This process is the result of a variety of factors . . . the growing disintegration of many families, the uncertainty of a time of "mutation" in which society, lacking a universally accepted ideal type, is in quest of its own future image of man; the voyeurism of a civilization which supplies

an abundance of information without corresponding possibilities for critical sifting of its value ... all these and many more factors militate against a well-balanced and harmonious growth into adulthood.[31]

The doctrine of the paschal mystery—that God changed the human prospect through the moral surrender of the God/man Jesus in his suffering and resurrection—has implications for a Christian perspective on moral development. It certainly means something for the parameters of moral-development theory.

The value of the negation of negativities needs to be affirmed. As I suggest above, there are many lives whose moral task is chiefly in the arena of courage and trust. No Christian moral-development theory can be allowed to lose or diminish the value of the moral surrender of one's loyalty and one's intelligence to the hidden force of divine love that makes it possible for invalids, incurables, and many others on the fringes of the social order to sustain life. The value of compassionate and trusting suffering eludes almost all of our rational categories. But experience teaches that, even in horizontal relationships between living persons, wounds teach something important about the wholeness of our humanity. Of the Savior the New Testament proclaims, "by his wounds you are healed." The theme of the negation of negativities would disclose the mystery that "by our wounds, others may be healed."[32] The power of an authentic compassion—one that has learned the lesson of the other's pain—is a moral force that must be included within the parameters of a Christian perspective on moral development.

Some persons will never become cheerful, postconventional persons.[33] Yet these same persons will be called into growth of various kinds. To do better justice to such persons and to reality itself, a serious task lies before moral education. It is the task of spelling out, with as much clarity as can be, the dimensions of moral striving and the stages of moral growth that touch the human experiences of courage, compassion, vocation, and faith. Here only part of the introduction to such a task is accomplished.

Some Tentative Conclusions

While the preceding pages present various critical perspectives that the Christian educator and theologian must bring to moral-development theory, in concluding it is necessary to acknowledge the indebtedness of the Christian moralist and educator to the work of Piaget, Kohlberg, Fowler, and their followers. The establishment of a field of empirical and theoretical research in moral development has made a difference in the way in which we perceive a number of problems and has contributed resources of importance, some of which ought to endure as tools for theology and religious education. In a very summary way, it is possible to indicate what moral-development theory contributes to theological ethics and moral education; likewise, it is possible to say in a few words what theological reflection promises to moral-development research.

The Counter-Reformation moral theology and catechetics in Catholicism promoted an almost static picture of human personality. By age seven, a child had reached the "age of reason" and so, as a creature endowed with reason and will, was imagined to be the responsible agent for a complex system of moral and religious duties. Though aided by grace to obey laws and customs in his society, still all the incapacities of a young person learning to adapt to the expectations of Christian society readily fell into the category of sins, and the moral energy of the Christian life focused upon denying oneself and doing one's duty.

Piaget's and Kohlberg's theories and research contribute a lot toward a more realistic and positive understanding of moral responsibility. By describing the plurality of moral stages through which growing persons pass and the dependence of more mature moral structures upon social understanding, moral-development theory places the legalistic mentality within its proper perspective as a limited and inadequate approach to moral understanding. There is probably no better cure for legalism or authoritarian attitudes than a quick course in moral-stage theory (something a great many teachers of adult courses have learned for themselves).

Second, Kohlberg's and Piaget's work helps us to understand the positive contribution of the lower stages. For centuries, Western civilization practically ignored the significance of the activities of infants previous to their acquisition of language. Piaget discovered that this early, prelinguistic period of human life is a time of enormous mental effort. Kohlberg's work, along with that of other researchers of developmental structures of cognition and personality, has succeeded in portraying a good deal of what children think and on what influences their thinking depends when confronted by moral decision. While much of the research still lies ahead of us, we are nonetheless fortunate so to have been directed to recognizing the importance of early stages of thinking and experience, where the foundations of symbolic thinking are the principal achievement of the work of development.

Third, both Piaget and Kohlberg have enriched moral discourse with the contribution of categories that allow us to situate problems of moral thinking and development with greater precision than we were previously able to do. The use of a term like Kohlberg's "postconventional level" allows one to evoke quickly and precisely quite a vast arrangement of ideas and connections that are important for ethical reflection. While previously an ethicist may have spoken of *epikeia,* an old Greek word used in ethics to speak of a capacity to make reasonable and responsible exceptions to rules, now in using the term *postconventional* one can associate that same capacity to see the exception to rules as reflecting a developmental advance related to social experience, to personal development, and to cognitive development.

Doubtless there will be other contributions of significance from moral-development theory to theological ethics, such as the importance of underlining the role of cognition in morality and the consequent re-examination of practical reason that this is beginning to stimulate. But these remarks suffice, for the present, to indicate that something of substance is at stake in the evolution of moral development as a field of research and theoretical learning.

The chief preoccupation of this article has been to suggest what theological reflection may offer to moral-development research. In referring to the Christian theology of creation, of the Holy Spirit, and of the Cross, I have tried to isolate some of the values that are affirmed as doctrinal commitments of a Christian theologian and teacher coming to moral education. On the basis of these observations, it seems clear that we can insist that faith is a distinct moral dimension present from childhood and developing in its own realm of activity; that moral agency develops from an inframoral heteronomy to a moral autonomy and into a supramoral heteronomy; and finally that much of moral experience is not merely the rational pursuit of the good, but the courageous negation of negativities.

To paraphrase Carl Rogers, "one out of every one of us is somehow wounded in our spirits." Each child must sustain the burden of separation from his or her mother at weaning, separation from the protective enclosure of the home at the time of schooling, and separation from supportive relationships within the nuclear family at adult independence. As Erikson has interpreted personal growth, each step toward maturity appears as a sort of balance within an uncollapsed tension: Erikson's "virtue" of fidelity is a balance between identity-diffusion derived from a plurality of relations and identity-formation derived essentially from inner evidence that comes from the self.[34]

Such perceptions manifest evidence of the shadowed side of human growth and of the inescapable tension that is the environment of growth. They provide a more balanced profile of moral development than does a concern with autonomous moral reasoning alone. While Erikson's research evidently sheds light on many aspects of human growth in a Christian context,[35] it may be that the doctrinal parameters which these pages have explored may demand some new departures.

Theological research into the nature and dimensions of moral development must begin to explore, I think, the subtle beginnings of religious experience and the positive contribution they make to the construction of a relational world. It needs to examine the implications of a charismatic heteronomy in spiritual adulthood. It needs, too, to articulate the structures of courage and hope, vocation and fidelity as they represent a rejection of destructiveness or a negation of negativities. Research of this kind will ground a developmental theory of autonomous moral rationality within a more holistic context. It will likewise respond to an agenda that Christian researchers can infer from their theological insights into revealed teaching.

Much of what has been written in recent years about discernment of spirits, pastoral psychology, and the theology of revelation may be helpful in beginning this work. Further, I should think that theological research into moral development and moral education would profit from a reexamination of certain things that medieval moral theory held about inner principles of moral acts, such as habits, virtues, and gifts of the Holy Spirit. While the contributions of the great moralists of the thirteenth and sixteenth centuries would have to be translated into categories and arguments that could dialogue with a new psychology of human action, such a conversation with the masters of the Christian past seems a welcome prospect. Kohlberg's intuition that moral development follows a *natural direction* inherent in the structure of the human has generated a new curiosity about how inner determinants of moral action operate. It was of that precisely that many of the medieval masters spoke.

Notes

1. L. Kohlberg, "Education, Moral Development and Faith," *Journal of Moral Education* 4, 1(1974), p. 15.

2. P. Rieff, "The Nature of Morality," No. 1 in the *Courses by Newspa-*

122   PAUL J. PHILIBERT

per of University Extension (Del Mar, Ca.: University of California, 1977), p. 4.

3. Kohlberg encourages this sense of despair, it seems to me, by demeaning the contributions which can be made by norms of politeness, the inculcation of virtue, and benevolent behavior management. I do not espouse any one of these items taken alone as the basis of a program for moral education; but then neither could I expect Kohlberg's moral-education strategies to be adequate apart from environmental and doctrinal influences.

4. P. Rieff, *op. cit.*

5. L. Kohlberg, "Foreword," in *Readings in Moral Education,* ed. P. Scharf (Minneapolis: Winston Press, 1978), p. 13.

6. P. J. Philibert, "Some Cautions on Kohlberg," *The Living Light* 12, 4(1975), pp. 530–2.

7. C. Bereiter, "The Morality of Moral Education," *Hastings Center Report* (April, 1978), p. 24.

8. P. Rieff, "Moral Education," No. 16 in the *Courses by Newspaper,* p. 44. Cf. n. 2.

9. Fowler's stages of faith incorporate Erikson's theory to a large extent. To the extent that this is so, Fowler's stages are more holistic than Kohlberg's stages; but likewise, Fowler's stage structure is less a stage-advance strategy for the same reason. See J. W. Fowler, "Stages in Faith: The Structural-Developmental Approach," in *Values and Moral Development,* ed. T. C. Hennessy (New York: Paulist Press, 1976), pp. 173–211.

10. Rieff's phrase in "Moral Education," *op. cit.,* p. 44, for Piaget's "centered thinking."

11. I find myself skeptical about the research-derivation of Kohlberg's stages when I put side by side two contrary data from Kohlberg's writings: (a) That Kohlberg extracted his characterization of the stages from his seventy-two boys in Chicago (L. Kohlberg, "A Cognitive-Developmental Approach to Moral Education," *The Humanist* [Nov.–Dec. 1972], p. 14), and (b) that he would no longer score any of his original group—in their initial interviews—at stage six (L. Kohlberg, "Continuities in Childhood and Adult Moral Development Revisited" in *Collected Papers on Moral Development and Moral Education* [Cambridge: Harvard School of Education, 1973], esp. p. 31). Where did the conceptualization of stage six come from, in that case?

12. L. Kohlberg, "Foreword" in *Readings in Moral Education,* pp. 2ff.

13. See, e.g., E. V. Sullivan, *Moral Learning* (New York: Paulist Press, 1975), pp. 95–120; P. J. Philibert, "Some Cautions on Kohlberg," *op. cit.* and "Conscience: Developmental Perspectives from Rogers and Kohlberg," *Horizons* 6, 1 (Spring, 1979), pp. 1–25.

14. B. Crittenden, *Form and Content in Moral Education.* Monograph Series, No. 12 (Toronto: Ontario Institute for Studies in Education, 1972), p. 23.

15. P. J. Philibert, "L. Kohlberg's Use of Virtue in His Theory of Mor-

al Development," *International Philosophical Quarterly* 15, 4(1975), pp. 455ff; K. Ryan, "Moral Formation: The American Scene" in *Moral Formation and Christianity*, eds. F. Bockle & J.-M. Pohier (New York: Seabury, 1978), pp. 103–5.

16. See, e.g., critiques by his colleagues in the field of psychology: W. Kurtines & E. B. Greif, "The Development of Moral Thought: Review and Evaluation of Kohlberg's Approach," *Psychological Bulletin* 81, 8(1974), pp. 453–470; E. L. Simpson, "Moral Development Research: A Case of Scientific Cultural Bias," *Human Development* 17, 2(1974), pp. 81–106; and E. V. Sullivan, *Kohlberg's Structuralism: A Critical Appraisal.* Monograph Series, No. 15 (Toronto: Ontario Institute for Studies in Education, 1977). An abstract of Sullivan's monograph can be found in Scharf's collection, *Readings in Moral Education*, pp. 272–82.

17. See J. C. Gibbs, "Kohlberg's Stages of Moral Judgment: A Constructive Critique," *Harvard Educational Review* 47, 1(1977), pp. 43–61. Cf. Simpson and Sullivan, *cit. supra.*

18. L. Kohlberg, "Education, Moral Development and Faith," p. 14.

19. *Summa Theologiae*, I, 104, 1.

20. A Biblical theology of *creation* would give an important place to the prophetic interpretation of God's fidelity to Israel during its O.T. captivity and return as a paradigm for our understanding of creative love. A passage like Isaiah 41:20, where the reconstitution of the exiled People is described with the conclusion, "the Holy One of Israel has created it," summarizes this attitude. God's fidelity is a creative, tenacious love, which punishes only to lead the beloved to the point of knowing that divine love cannot be negotiated or bought; the freedom and unconditional quality of divine benevolence appear precisely when they are offered to the destitute. See, e.g., G. Trenkler, "Creation" in *Sacramentum Verbi*, vol. I, ed. J. B. Bauer (New York: Herder & Herder, 1970), pp. 147–155; and P. Auvray, "Creation" in *Dictionary of Biblical Theology*, ed. X. Léon-Dufour (New York: Seabury Press, 1973), pp. 98–102.

21. L. Kohlberg, "Education, Moral Development and Faith," p. 14.

22. P. J. Philibert, "Conscience: Developmental Perspectives from Rogers and Kohlberg."

23. L. Kohlberg, *idem.*

24. L. Kohlberg, "From Is to Ought: How to Commit the Naturalistic Fallacy and Get Away With It in the Study of Moral Development," in *Cognitive Development and Epistemology*, ed. T. Mischel (New York: Academic Press, 1971), pp. 214–5.

25. See Sullivan, *Kohlberg's Structuralism*, pp. 12ff; especially p. 13: "Is morality simply the development of a system of social arrangements that can deal with conflicts of interest in an ideal and disinterested way? If this is so, can a society or community be said to be based on a moral system if man at his deepest level is assumed to enter into social arrangements simply out of conflicts of interest?"

26. L. Kohlberg, "From Is to Ought," p. 215.

27. M. Schmaus, "Holy Spirit: Pneumatology," in *Encyclopedia of Theology,* the Concise Sacramentum Mundi, ed. K. Rahner (New York: Seabury Press, 1975), p. 644.

28. L. Monden, *Sin, Liberty and Law,* trans. J. Donceel (New York: Sheed & Ward, 1965), pp. 8–9. The existence of a supramoral heteronomy is an idea explored by Tillich in various places. See, e.g., his suggestions for a "theonomous ethics" in his *Theology of Culture* (New York: Oxford University Press, 1959), pp. 133–45. Similar clues for an understanding of this theme occur in K. Rahner's "theology of childhood" where the attribute of being "a child of God" entails an orientation to God which expresses "trustful submission to control by another, the courage to allow fresh horizons . . . a readiness to journey into the untried and the untested" and all this within a transcendent relationship of faith, hope and love. See K. Rahner, "Ideas for a Theology of Childhood" in *Theological Investigations,* vol. VIII, trans. D. Bourke (New York: Herder & Herder, 1971), p. 48.

29. The stages along this dimension are another matter, although it is not inept to comment here that one characterization of that development is from animistic/anthropomorphic images through physical/structural images into metaphysical/mystical images of God experience. Cf. J. W. Fowler, "Stages in Faith" in *Values and Moral Development.* Since we postulate, on the basis of our theological reflection, infantile stages of religious experience (I wish to avoid the use of the term "preconventional" here to describe these stages), of course there would be a kind of "heteronomy of deference to the Holy Spirit" all along the developmental structure of *religion/faith.* To talk of movement from heteronomy to autonomy to a charismatic and theologically grounded heteronomy, then, is to demand an elaboration of the interrelationship between social operations (adult autonomy) and private religious experience (supramoral heteronomy).

30. See Sullivan, *Kohlberg's Structuralism;* also, E. L. Simpson, "Moral Development Research: A Case of Scientific Cultural Bias."

31. L. Monden, *Sin, Liberty and Law,* pp. 28–29.

32. See I Peter 2:24. This theme has been fruitfully explored by H. Nouwen in several of his writings. See, e.g., *The Wounded Healer* (Garden City, N.Y.: Doubleday, 1972) and *Reaching Out* (Garden City, N.Y.: Doubleday, 1975).

33. A powerful and thoughtful reflection on this theme can be found in L. Beirnaert, "Does Sanctity Depend on Psychic Structure?" *Cross Currents* (Winter, 1951), pp. 39ff.

34. See E. H. Erikson, *Insight and Responsibility* (New York: Norton, 1964), pp. 111ff. Also E. H. Erikson, *Identity: Youth and Crisis* (New York: Norton, 1968), pp. 91–141.

35. Several authors have explored this contribution of Erikson's theories to pastoral reflection. See, e.g., D. S. Browning, *Generative Man* (New York: Dell Publishing Co., 1975); B. McLaughlin, *Nature, Grace and Reli-*

gious Development (New York: Paulist Press, 1963)—now unfortunately out of print; and G. Fourez, *The End of the Taboos* (Philadelphia: Fortress Press, 1973).

I am indebted to several colleagues for helpful discussion in preparing these pages—most particularly to my colleague, Dr. Mark Heath, who kindly read and criticized an earlier draft.

Beyond Hunger:
Toward a Food First Ethic

William J. Wood

Introduction

This paper is principally a theological reflection on the work of Frances Moore Lappé, Joseph Collins, and their colleagues of the Institute for Food and Development Policy.[1] I am personally indebted to them—and deeply grateful—for their time, attention, advice and encouragement.

Coming to live with *FOOD FIRST: Beyond the Myth of Scarcity* has been a profoundly liberating experience for me, as I know it has been and will be for countless others. I suspect that my reflections will take on much more meaning if one has read *FOOD FIRST*. There is no way I could communicate in a brief paper the full impact of a work of 466 carefully written pages. I hope that I have not in any way distorted the book.

As dependent as this paper is on the work of Dr. Collins and Ms. Lappé, I must take full responsibility for any mistakes or shortcomings.

To provide a framework for my reflections, I have drawn generously from Denis Goulet, a pioneer in the ethics of development.[2] I agree with him that the moral questions societies faced in the past have become acutely contemporary development questions, which means that ethicists, if they are to avoid sterile moralism, need developmentalists; while developmentalists, if they are to find answers to the normative questions that they are faced with, need ethicists. And so, I feel that I am on a right track in seeking to develop ethical strategies for combatting world hunger in dialogue with the Institute for Food and Development Policy. That they have assembled the very best collection of development research and analysis only makes the enterprise more valuable and exciting.

I. Hunger: Phenomenon and Symptom

Not too long ago I had the good fortune of living for a year with a religious community just outside the tiny town of Wépion in Belgium. Although we were mostly a community of students and professors, all of us helped out a little on the fifteen-acre farm on which we lived. Almost everything we ate and drank was grown on our farm. The brother cook would pick the vegetables each day before dinner. Breakfast milk for our *café au lait* came from our own cows, as did the butter and soft cheese. We baked whole-grain bread. None of our food was processed and refined. The little meat we ate was quite lean, from grass-fed animals. There wasn't a great abundance, but there was enough, and it was delicious and nourishing. I lost twenty pounds that year, without dieting. No one talked of diets or vitamins and minerals and minimum daily requirements. No one counted calories and carbohydrates, nor did we worry about cholesterol and polyunsaturated fats. *We had control over our own food.* Nor do I recall television commercials for food—junk or otherwise.

It occurs to me that food was much like that when I was growing up during the 30's and 40's in Reading, Pennsylvania. Though we weren't farmers, we had farms all around us. And those who did not live on farms cultivated "victory gardens" during the war. People were closer to their food. *People had control over their food!*

Of course, not everyone in the world had control over his or her food forty years ago. We had heard of Ireland's potato famine. And we always had to finish off our peas, mindful of the poor starving children in China. The social and political forces that create hunger had been building up for a long time before then, though we did not start using the term *world hunger* until some years later. Europe was hungry for a while at the end of the war. But organizations such as the Red Cross and Oxfam provided food relief, while the people of the United States, through the Marshall Plan, helped the countries of Europe to rebuild themselves and *to take control once again of their own food.*

Through different means, not to be judged in this paper, the legendary hungry masses of China—numbering almost a billion—took control over their food, too. In less than twenty-five years they wiped chronic hunger from their country.

In most of the rest of the world, however, hunger is a more deadly reality than it was forty years ago. Both undernutrition and malnutrition abound.[3] The latest figures of the Food and Agriculture Organization of the United Nations (FAO) reveal that there are over 400 million undernourished people in the developing nations.[4] The numbers of malnourished are much more difficult to calculate, since so many die before they can be counted. But the FAO notes that malnutrition results from more than simply a lack of food. It is found particularly in the poorest countries, *in the poorest sections of the urban population and in rural areas where land-tenure systems and other factors lead to the emergence of large land-less and unemployed groups.*

Hunger cannot be justly considered in isolation, or its most profound significance will never be understood. Hungry people are not simply hungry. They live in gross conditions of underdevelopment. They lack essential goods. Their lives are controlled by alien forces. Their basic rights are brutally repressed. Hunger is the most obvious symptom of the disease that eats at their lives. They have no control over their food system, their lives, their destiny.

The same disease besets those who are not obviously hungry (though many may be malnourished in their obesity).[5] Erich Fromm speaks of the alienation in mindless affluence that is just as dehumanizing as the alienation of the desperately poor.[6] The core of the phenomenon of hunger is dehumanization. We are not just talking about herds of cattle that have no food. We are talking about hundreds of millions of *human persons* who are forced to live desperately and die painfully, in a manner unbefitting the lowest of animals.

Nor is hunger a place. Ten million people are hungry in the United States, the richest country the world has ever known. And 36 million of our people live below the poverty level. They, too, have no control over their food or over their destiny. One out of every ten persons in the United States is a senior citizen, most living on fixed incomes. Hunger and malnutrition affect older people more than any other segment of our population. The problem is not just their hunger. It is their loneliness, lack of mobility, dehumanization. Many eat pet food because they cannot afford human food.

II. Why Are People Hungry?

In a sense, the answer to this question is very simple, although it has been spun into such a complex web of myth and make-believe that most Americans, even "experts," are unable to see it. *HUNGER IS CREATED BY HUMAN-MADE ECONOMIC SYSTEMS THAT DETERMINE HOW RESOURCES ARE USED AND FOR WHOSE BENEFIT!* Hungry people are the logical consequence of the economic system that, in all its complexity, puts more and more control of our world into the hands of fewer and fewer people.

The staff of the Institute for Food and Development Policy, in the unfinished draft of a forthcoming booklet,[7] has pinpointed six elements of an economic system that generate hunger even amidst plenty. These six economic "givens" are extremely helpful eye-openers. I will give just a brief indication of the "givens" here, to aid in discerning the root causes of world hunger.

(1) *PRODUCTIVE RESOURCES ARE USED EXCLUSIVELY AS A SOURCE OF PRIVATE GAIN.* The "extra" produced by workers beyond their survival needs is used by those in control for private consumption and expansion, not for the needs of the community as a whole. For example, wealth produced by $1.20 a day plantation workers in the Philippines goes to benefit local elites and Del Monte executives and stockholders, not the banana workers themselves. Which would not be so bad, *if* everyone had virtually equal control over productive resources. But, owing to another "given," they do not.

(2) *THERE IS INEQUALITY IN CONTROL OVER PRODUCTIVE RESOURCES.* Where productive resources are controlled by individuals, each person's attempt to maximize his or her gain leads to extreme inequality in assets. Those with a slight edge—richer land, access to credit, ability to absorb losses of a bad season, etc.—expand, eliminating competitors from control over resources. This happened to tomato farmers in California after 1965 when only 20 percent of them could afford to invest in the newly developed tomato-picking machine.[8] In the United States, 5.5 percent of all farms control more than 50 percent of all farmland, while, on a worldwide basis, 80 percent of the land is owned by 3 percent of the people.

The fewer the people in control of society's assets, the easier it is for these few to determine how much of the "extra" wealth gets returned to the workers who produce it, and how much remains in their control. Where a few landholders own most of the land, for example, they can keep wages down and prices up—and even eliminate jobs altogether by replacing people with machines.

(3) *PRODUCTION OF WHAT SELLS AT THE GREATEST PROFIT, NOT WHAT IS NEEDED.* Scarcity of basic items comes to coexist with a proliferation of nonessentials, because production is geared to those who have the most money to spend. In Northwest Mexico thousands of landless laborers suffer from malnutrition, while the land they work grows grapes for brandy or tomatoes for the highest paying urban and foreign markets. And in Brazil, oranges are exported to the United States while vitamin C deficiency afflicts millions there.

(4) *ECONOMIC DECISIONS BASED SOLELY ON PRESENT PROFITABILITY TO THE INDIVIDUAL.* The demand for immediate returns does not allow for long-term planning that is critical in agriculture. Soil is not allowed to lie fallow and replenish its natural fertility. Crops are not rotated to restore the soil. Chemical fertilizers and pesticides will be used more heavily to upset nature's balance. Each grower's attempt to reap maximum profit today risks undercutting the agricultural resources needed to produce food in the future and results in periodic overproduction in relation to what people can buy.

(5) *ECONOMIC DECISIONS MADE AT THE TOP.* The concentration of economic power suppresses people's socially creative energies. As more and more farmers lose their land, here and abroad, they become at best tenants, sharecroppers or laborers. Having no control over the land they work and no assurance that their labor will benefit them, motivation to improve and protect the land is severely undermined.

(6) *THOSE IN CONTROL OF PRODUCTIVE RESOURCES ARE ALSO IN CONTROL OF PUBLIC ATTENTION.* Those at the pinnacle of the economic system control all forms of communications and advertising. A glance at some advertising budgets for 1976 provides a clue as to *how* large corporations control the media: Kool-Aid $13,200,000; McDonald's $105,000,000; Mars, Inc. $40,850,000; Kellogg $67,200,000; General Foods $275,000,000 (yes, that's millions); Coca-Cola $91,300,000; Wonder Bread $4,437,000; Sugar Frosted Flakes $4,726,100; Cap'n Crunch $4,200,000.[9] Rather than responding to people's needs or being concerned with nutrition, the major food firms can actually create desires according to which products bring them the greatest profits.

In the face of these six elements of our economic system, is it any wonder that the majority of people in the world have no control over the most basic part of their lives: whether they shall eat, what they shall eat, how much of a share they shall have of what they produce, what is done to the food they can afford, how much it shall cost to eat? Hunger—undernutrition and malnutrition—is the most blatant result of such "givens." Dehumanization is the more profound and universal result.

In brief, the most fundamental reason why millions are hungry is an unjust and ineffective social and economic system.

The Complexity of World Hunger

The world food system is, after all, a system, itself containing many subsystems. There are no "single-factor solutions," though single-factor analysis can be very helpful. Many different contingencies and issues are involved in the production, delivery and consumption of food: some "actors," for example, are farmers, farmworkers, input suppliers, food processors, wholesale brokers and distributors, and retailers. Issues arise from a diversity of elements in a food system: for example, patterns of land control, water resources, energy, marketing, credit and banking interests, nutrition, corporate penetration of institutional food systems, governmental policies and legislation, international trade, technology and mechanization, pest control, environment, rural development, increased urbanization and industrialization, etc.

Unfortunately, however, complexity is often used as an excuse for refusing to face issues, a spawning-bed for maldirecting or paralyzing myths, or a ruse to keep people from participating in decision-making. After all, it's so complex that only the "experts" can deal with it.

The strands of the system, in all its complexity, can be woven together so as to depict the nature of the system. This is being done by a number of people, and a fairly clear picture is emerging. The picture reveals that, of all the many factors of the world food system, the ones that are crucial for eradicating hunger are the sociopolitical and economic ones.

More significant than the complexity of the food system, however, is the fact that the generation of hunger (and thus its eradication) is a *historical process*, not a static phenomenon. No one fully understands it yet. No one knows all the answers to it. As we work with what we already know toward the solution of world hunger, we need to keep seeking fuller answers. If hunger, as the best analysis reveals, is not an aberration but the systemic product of historical forces, then answers will come only as part of an historical process long enough to alter systems. But we do not have to be passive victims of history. We can influence the motion that is there, more and more consciously influencing the creation of new forms.

III. Hunger as a Metaphysical Problem

Have not human beings permitted, nay, even induced the development of hunger and outrageous inequality because of a distorted vision of human nature and of human relationships? What else caused the "Holocaust"? E. F. Schumacher gets to the core:

> In the excitement over the unfolding of his scientific and technical powers, modern man has built a system of production that ravishes nature and a type of society that mutilates man. If only there were more and more wealth, everything else, it is thought, would fall into place. Money is considered to be all-powerful; if it could not actually buy nonmaterial values, such as justice, harmony, beauty or even health, it could circumvent the need for them or compensate for their loss. The development of production and the acquisition of wealth have thus become the highest goals of the modern world in relation to which all other goals, no matter how much lip service may still be paid to them, have come to take second place. The highest goals require no justification; all secondary goals have finally to justify themselves in terms of the service their attainment renders to the attainment of the highest.[10]

With Schumacher, we see this metaphysic of materialism being challenged by events. The "logic of production" is not the logic of life or of society. "Not by bread alone does man live," Jesus replied to the Tempter who invited him to produce bread from stones. People are beginning to grasp the importance of these words in a new way. They are becoming increasingly aware that to live by the acquisition of wealth alone is a sure way to destroy life. Even planners and "experts" are finally coming to admit that development is not merely a matter of increasing per-capita income. The bankruptcy of this policy is only too evident in many third-world countries where an exaggerated concentration on economic factors has led to the growth of poverty rather than to its diminution. Hence the importance of the approach that puts people first and looks at their real and human needs.

The process can start only with people, where they are, with them participating fully in everything. People have a right to the disposal of the land where they live. The resources of society belong to the people.

A materialistic metaphysic puts things before people. It is the same philosophy that allowed slavery to continue for so long. We have advanced beyond slavery and now perhaps we are ready to abandon the metaphysic that supported it. Will the day come when we will look on the notion of "food for profit" with as much disdain as we now regard slavery? Will the day come when "food" will regain its intrinsic person-related significance? When we begin to value food as first and foremost for people, then will we be able to eradicate hunger.

For now, however, because the materialistic metaphysic has been built into social relationships and economic structures, the most pressing question is: What kind of structures of human organization can we help create that will lead to "food-first-for-people" as a policy?

IV. Eradicating Hunger

How the Problem Has Been Approached

The ethical system permeating American culture since the colonies first won their fight for independence has been a strange amalgamation of the Protestant work ethic, the pursuit-of-self-interest-as-good Smithian ethic, and the Renaissance-bred humanistic ethic of egalitarianism and benevolence.[11]

Still underlying the attitude of some Americans toward the hungry, particularly those of their own country, is the feeling that these people are poor because they are lazy. Those who feel this way bemoan the use of their taxes to support people who refuse to work. After all, "my daddy worked his way up from nothing—why can't they?" This approach, though not generally thought out to its logical conclusion, would solve the problem of hunger by rewarding (e.g., through tax breaks) those who produce more, and by ceasing to reward (through welfare and aid programs) those who do not produce.

The Smithian ethic clearly underlines our competitive, capitalistic economic system, as well as the predominant socio-cultural attitude of the American people. The "do your own thing" mentality is in the same spirit. God—or some unnamed force—somehow weaves individual self-interested endeavors into a common good. In pursuing self-interest, we simultaneously serve the needs of others. Cooperative arrangements in pursuit of self-interest become a good investment, as well as an act of assistance.

The approach of this ethic to world hunger is to increase production and expand marketing in the belief that, although the primary motive is bigger and bigger profits, the side effects will serve the needs of the hungry by increasing employment, raising the standard of living in poverty-stricken areas, and making more products available. Thus, the Nestlé, S.A., Company boasts that it has been taking positive steps to improve both poverty and hunger since it entered the third world in 1921. It "now has more than eighty-one plants manufacturing a wide variety of food products in twenty-five 'third world' countries. More than thirty-six thousand local employees work in those facilities. Nestlé views industrial development as a major factor in raising the standard of living in poverty-stricken areas."[12]

Inequality is part of the social vision of Smithian ethics. The benefit to the poor from the exclusive pursuit of self-interest is, at best, an illusion. In fact, the more multinational corporations have penetrated developing countries, the poorer and hungrier the people have become.

The reason for that, according to the neo-Malthusian ethic, is population growth in developing countries outstrips even the highly advanced productive capacities of modern technology and the multinational corporate investments. The poor tend to breed without limits. Thus, as Garret Hardin rearticulates in his "lifeboat" ethics,[13] to give the poor increased amounts of food only results in increasing the numbers of the poor. Other versions of this neo-Malthusianism stress the depletion of natural resources with its resultant scarcity. The social vision of all the versions, however, is totally pessimistic.

In response to hunger, "lifeboat" ethics and its look-alikes call for withholding charity as the most humane action, as well as the most responsible. At the same time, they see intensive measures to decrease population growth as the only hope for the survival of our planet.

To be quite frank, such a simplistic reductionism so defies common sense that refuting it would be a waste of time, except for the mind-boggling fact that the majority of popular thinking and a great deal of the ethical analysis of world hunger are founded on the unfounded presuppositions of neo-Malthusianism! Perhaps the reason for this is tied in with the metaphysics of hunger. "In a very real way the world *looks* like an image of what man believes about himself."[14] The very question of the value of life itself is at stake here. To say that no one has a right to exist unless he or she exists in optimal circumstances removes our challenge to improve our lot and our world, a challenge given in each birth. "Indeed . . . the world's chief resource is the population and the human capital thus represented. As long as there is no limit to human knowledge, there is no limit to any of the other resources that make up this universe."[15]

Philosophical considerations apart, however, "lifeboat" ethics sinks because it simply is not based on the facts. Is it not obvious that today large areas of the world such as Western Europe, Russia and China are more populous than ever before and yet the majority of people are eating better than in any previous generation? How can an overpopulation theory be reconciled with the fact that some of the areas of the world that are among the least dense and have among the slowest growing populations, such as the United States and West Germany, represent the greatest drain on the world's finite resources?[16]

Neither population growth nor the size of today's population is the cause of hunger. On the other hand, it has been established that the insecurity of hunger and desperate poverty is the principal cause of overpopulation. With the authors of *FOOD FIRST,* I do not contend that overpopulation is not a problem. I do contend that overpopulation is not the cause of world hunger, nor even a major factor in the making of hunger at this time.

Humanistic ethics of various kinds have, from the beginning, been interwoven in America with the work ethic and the philosophy of Adam Smith. Americans have traditionally been generous and benevolent, desirous of minimizing human suffering. At the same time that we were allowing a system to be constructed that militated against this, we believed that those who have should give to the less privileged in order to attain a greater equality within society. Guided by this ethic, from both private and public funds we created institutions that cared for the disabled, orphaned or otherwise disadvantaged.

The main thrust of this ethic is "charity." And Americans have contributed more to "charity" than, probably, any other national grouping. Which makes it understandable that the most common American approach to world hunger is to make donations to relief agencies. Millions of dollars are contributed privately by Americans each year for various feeding programs at home and abroad.

Without being cynical, but to illustrate the intermixture of Smithian and humanistic ethics, it can be pointed out that contributions to charitable agencies are, generally, tax-deductible.

The Marxian ethic has not been very strong in the United States, for obvious reasons. But its proponents have increased in recent decades. And in some ways it is so similar to biblically based ethics that unidentified quotations from papal encyclicals have been judged as coming from the pen of Karl Marx. The Marxian ethic views human history as a struggle between the "haves" and the "have nots," with the highest good being social justice. It envisions the fought-for eventuality of an egalitarian society, in which all work is equally rewarded and all privilege abolished. Being socially responsible means aligning ourselves with the oppressed in support of their struggle.

The Marxist approach to world hunger would be to overthrow by revolution the oppressive structures that make the rich richer and the poor hungrier. Marx would not have much patience with incremental change of structure.

Obviously, all these descriptions of ethical systems are oversimplified. But they may give a "feel" for the various approaches to world hunger taken by Americans, and how those approaches can be intermingled, sometimes even contradictorily.

Toward A Food First Ethic

> God created man in the image of himself, in the image of God he created him, male and female he created them.
>
> God blessed them, saying to them, "Be fruitful, multiply, fill the earth and conquer it. Be masters of the fish of the sea, the birds of heaven and all living animals on the earth." God said, "See, I give you all the seed-bearing plants that are on the whole earth, and all the trees with seed-bearing fruit; this shall be your food."
>
> (Gen. 1:27–29)

The end, the value of values, is the human person, male and female, made in the image of God, born free to be masters of the earth.

And to sustain that sacred human life in all its dignity what comes first? Food. All the resources of the earth are entrusted as gift to human beings that they may have food, first.

Is it mere coincidence that the "fall" of the human race, with its consequent alienation of creation from its Creator, should be portrayed as abuse of food? Is it mere coincidence that Cain should kill his brother Abel over food—food to be recognized as a sacred gift of God? Is it mere coincidence that Jacob should become Israel, heir to the promise made to Abraham and Isaac, by giving his food—a mess of pottage—to his older brother, Esau? Is it mere coincidence that Yahweh should have his people sit down to a meal—food first—before setting out on the long, desert road to freedom; and that he should nourish them along the way (when they longed for the meat they had eaten as slaves) with the manna from heaven.

As the Passover meal is central to the Jew, so the Eucharistic meal is central to the Christian. And the one criterion that Jesus solemnly proclaimed as determining his Last Judgment on human beings was whether or not they had fed the hungry. Food first—and last!

No ethic can lead to the ultimate solution, ultimate salvation. All things will be finally reconciled only in Jesus Christ, only in the Parousia. Food is not an absolute value, no more than justice, peace and freedom are absolute values. Ethical strategies to end hunger are not strategies to induce the Parousia. Nevertheless, Christians are mandated to incarnate God in the flesh of human history, to make history, to build up the Kingdom, to be creative architects of new possibilities, "redeeming the present." As Denis Goulet reminds us, the divine summons to bear witness to transcendence does not exempt us from the divine summons to make history, regardless of the tension between the two summonses.

> In order to make history they [Christians] must recognize that underdevelopment, and the train of evils which go in its wake, are not *necessary* evils decreed by gods or assigned by nature, but human creations flowing from sinfulness, exploitation, ignorance, privilege. There is not, nor can there ever be, any warrant for Christian resignation in the face of stubbornly persistent structures of injustice, dehumanizing poverty, and humiliating domination. To resist these structures and to replace them with others which promote greater justice and dignity in the access to goods and their distribution, empowerment in important spheres of decision—this is what it means to make history and to transform oppressed peoples into veritable *subjects*, not mere *objects* of their social destiny.[17]

The general end to which any biblical or stewardship ethic will be directed is the fullness of human life for each and every human person, and all human persons together (which is really the same thing), living in union with God as sons and daughters created in his image. This is justice—for the earth and its inhabitants to be right with God.

In the concrete situation of world hunger, an organizing ethical principle will see "food first" as the end to be achieved, recognizing the full personal and spiritual implications of "food." Getting food into hungry people's mouths is not the heart of the matter. As Pope Paul expressed it:

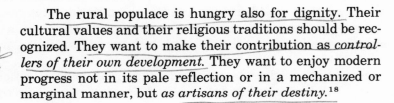

> The rural populace is hungry also for dignity. Their cultural values and their religious traditions should be recognized. They want to make their contribution as *controllers of their own development.* They want to enjoy modern progress not in its pale reflection or in a mechanized or marginal manner, but as *artisans of their destiny.*[18]

That is why mere relief or feeding programs are not the solution at all, needed as they may be as patchwork or temporary measures until the problem is got to at its roots. What is at stake is not being fed, it is meaning, exercise of basic human rights, justice, freedom, dignity, control over one's own life, humanization. A food first ethic will go beyond hunger to living-in-human-dignity as its goal, acknowledging that the betrayal of that human dignity is most vividly concretized in hunger, in not having control over the most fundamental of human needs, food.

The authors of *FOOD FIRST* list ten fundamentals of food self-reliance that specify more concretely the goals for which a food first ethic will strive:[19]

(1) Every country in the world has the resources necessary for its people to free themselves from hunger.

(2) To balance the planet's population and resources, we must now address the root cause of both hunger and high birth rates: the insecurity and poverty of the majority that results from the control over basic national resources by a few.

(3) Hunger is only made worse when approached as a technical problem. Hunger can only be overcome by the transformation of social relationships in which the major-

ity directly participate in building a democratic economic system.

(4) Political and economic inequalities are the greatest stumbling block to development.

(5) Safeguarding the world's agricultural environment and people freeing themselves from hunger are complementary goals.

(6) Agriculture must become, first and foremost, a way for people to produce the food they need and secondarily a possible source of foreign exchange.

(7) Our food security is not threatened by hungry people but by a system that concentrates economic power into the hands of elites who profit by the generation of scarcity and the internationalization of food control.

(8) Today, in every country in the world, people are working to democratize the control over food-producing resources.

(9) Escape from hunger comes not through the redistribution of food but only through the redistribution of control over food-producing resources.

(10) For Americans distressed about the reality of hunger in a world of plenty, the tasks ahead are clear: Work to remove those obstacles preventing people from taking charge of their food-producing resources—obstacles that today are being built by our government, by U.S.–supported international agencies, and U.S.–based corporations. Our work toward food self-reliance and democratization of our own economy allies us with the struggle of people in underdeveloped countries fighting for food self-determination.

But even concretized ends are not enough. An ethic, if it is to make any contribution to the reconstruction of the social order, must go "beyond moralism," as Denis Goulet has insisted. Ethics must become *praxis*. To do so genuinely, ethics must continually strive to become "a 'means of the means,' i.e., a critical reflection on concrete measures leading to effective transformations of an oppressive socio-economic structure."[20] Sister Marie Augusta Neal, as she proposes a "theology of relinquishment," suggests that the essential concrete measure to be taken by first-world people facing third-world peoples who are struggling for liberation is to let go.[21] This is the unspoken theme of what follows.

"Letting Go": Strategies for Change

U.S. farmers may not start a revolution,[22] but they can well be part of effective change strategies, working in the mode of creative evolutionary change. The farmers are likely to win the support of consumers and of a diversity of people working within the food system. In the light of what is already happening in North America, as well as what can be made to happen, I suggest five essential ingredients of an effective change strategy: (1) Liberation of self-confidence by increased consciousness of individual and collective power; (2) An ongoing process of education and evaluation; (3) Collaboration and division of labor; (4) Identifying strategic social forces and institutional leverage points; (5) Sustained commitment.

(1) Increased Consciousness of Power

A paralyzing fear grips many people when they are confronted with the myths of world hunger. One of the unspoken myths, of course, is that ordinary people are powerless. So we are made to feel guilty and helpless to do anything about that for which we feel guilty. The fear-ridden guilt moves to despair rather than responsibility. Even when we have broken through the other myths, the reality seems even more overwhelmingly hopeless than the mythical version. We feel powerless and puny, like David before Goliath. "The greatest danger facing Christian social change agents today is clearly the loss of hope."[23] How do we become aware of our power?

The poet claims that bars do not a prison make. Nor does the absence of bars constitute freedom. Freedom—from fear, fruitless guilt, helplessness, hopelessness, powerlessness—comes from letting go. It is discovered, taken. David would never have conquered Goliath if he were not convinced that he could do it.

Only those who have confidence that they can effect change will effect change.

Where is this liberated self-confidence to come from? Christians talk about "metanoia," although not usually in this context. "Metanoia" means a radical transformation of mind and heart, with emphasis, however, more often placed on change of heart (from selfishness and greed, for example, to altruism and generosity). But the Greek word itself denotes transformation of mind (or mindset)—from blindness and ignorance to perception and knowledge. "The Truth shall make you free."

The more one learns about the initially overwhelming forces generating hunger, the more one sees them as the work of finite human beings, a work that can be transformed by finite human beings, just as the power of Goliath—for all its immensity—could be undone by puny little David.

Our self-confidence becomes even more liberated when we discover that people not only *can* effect radical change in the face of overwhelming odds, but that they *have done so* and *are doing so* today.[24]

Only as enough people become confident about their ability to change the way things are will any change strategy be effective.

(2) Ongoing Process of Education and Evaluation

It was well over a year ago that Joseph Collins and Frances Lappé were warning us that most of what we read in the future would not reflect the reality they tried to convey in *FOOD FIRST*. How right they were. The myths are indeed deeply imbedded. It is so easy to read a Peter Huessy[25] and wallow nostalgically in that old feeling of despair, waiting helplessly for doomsday. One allows oneself to be trapped into a radio debate on whether anti-abortionists stand in the way of solving world hunger. An enthusiastic article temptingly titled "A New Perception of World Hunger"[26] almost leads one to overlook the fact that the article is based on the old misperception that increased production is all that is needed to solve world hunger. All the myths keep popping up again and again, often from the mouths and pens of so-called experts.

The most obvious truth loses cognitive plausibility when the majority of people are unaware of it. And so, the social-change agent needs to make his own education an ongoing process. The complexities of hunger, along with the fact that it is a dynamic and not a static reality, also calls for continuing education as essential to any change strategy.

Moreover, whatever one is doing to effect change must be regularly evaluated, since incremental measures readily reduce themselves to palliatives. And palliative measures, as Dennis Goulet so well observes, block real change, deceiving people in the process. Eventually, palliatives actually make things worse. "They give birth to hopes they cannot satisfy or tinker with failing social mechanisms, thereby postponing treatment until the disease becomes incurable."[27]

From an understanding of the nature of the problem and of what is necessary to address it, several criteria emerge by which one can judge any action attempting to eradicate hunger: (a) Does the action expose the fact that elements we take for granted in our economic system inevitably bring about inequality and suffering?

(b) Does the action provide an alternative to the dominant system? That is, does it represent a change in structure, or at least a step in that direction? (c) Does the action make clear that ordinary people can work together to change things and to achieve greater self-determination? (d) Does the action lay the foundation (or plant a seed) for further action? That is, does it, by its own internal process, expand future possibilities or is it just "a one-shot affair"?

The range of actions that could be pursued is virtually unlimited—from supporting hunger relief, organizing a food co-op, or establishing a community garden; through boycotting Nestlé, lobbying for or against legislation, joining the farmers' strike, making an educational film or devising some sort of simulation game, working for land reform locally, or participating in a "Peoples' Food Commission"; to . . . you name it. Often enough the same kind of action could constitute, depending on subjective and objective intention and circumstances, an obstacle to the end of hunger, a palliative measure, or a genuine contribution to the eradication of hunger. Periodic evaluation, therefore (with revision when called for), is essential for any change strategy to be effective.

(3) People Working Together

One of the most effective techniques of "brainwashing" is to isolate individuals from their companions. "It is not good for man to be alone," says the Book of Genesis. No one person built the structures that generate hunger, and no one person can transform those structures to enable people to feed themselves.

Perhaps the greatest reason for optimism about world hunger is the fact that literally thousands of individuals and hundreds of groups are working together to get at the causes of hunger. Some are researching; some are creatively communicating the results of research; many are acting on the results of the research in a myriad of different ways.

Nothing can substitute for the support and power that comes from laboring alongside others who share the same vision and the same determination. Effective change requires collaboration.

It also requires division of labor. No one can be involved in every aspect of what is needed in the fight against hunger. Individuals can be helped to discern the forms their energies might take by examining their own situation (who are they? where are they? how much time do they have? whom do they want to reach? with whom can they link up? etc.). A potential change agent can be thwarted or burnt out either by trying to do too much or by launching into a project for which he is not suited by temperament or talent.

One type of action, however, virtually everyone can engage in, i.e., the exercise of responsible citizenship. That is one reason why Bread for the World, a Christian citizens' movement, can be so appealing to the ordinary person. Furthermore, Bread for the World, whose members already number over twenty thousand, has revealed the power of people working together as evidenced by legislation passed in response to Bread for the World letter campaigns.

(4) Exploiting Institutional Leverage Points

Not only do people need to work together, the "right" people need to be brought into the action. "No change strategy is conceivable without identifying the social forces which can implement it."[28] Denis Goulet suggests that new alliances may be needed for more comprehensive social change in the United States: radical politicized militants, dissident technocrats and bureaucrats, social prophets speaking to and for religious constituencies, critical intellectuals, and a mass base of "ordinary" American interest groups (workers, oppressed minorities and women, the ethnically marginalized).

Both in businesses and in schools, one is likely to have more of an "in" by cultivating the secretary than by cultivating the boss or dean. The point is that there are certain key personnel in any operation, and there are key positions from which action is more likely to be effective.

The effective change agent will identify those people and those positions. Interestingly, many of the contingencies Dennis Goulet suggests are already allying in the food movement in the United States and Canada. The People's Food Commission based in Ottawa, for example, is made up of workers, farmers, church groups, agricultural marketing groups, international agencies such as Oxfam, labor unions, fishermen, and citizen coalitions.[29] A burgeoning California Food Policy Project has assembled under one roof government officials, farmers, consumer advocates, critical intellectuals (mostly ethicists), nutritionists, agricultural researchers; representatives of United Farm Workers, Bread for the World, Safeway, the Northern California Grocers' Association, and even multinational corporations (Standard Oil, Del Monte, Fleming, Castle and Cook).

As such individuals and groups reflect and work together, they must be constantly alert to "detect, or create, institutional leverage points whence they may contribute to overall change. This they can do either by solving problems in a mode of creative incrementalism, or by seizing favorable opportunities to introduce abrupt discontiuities in oppressive social structures."[30] This latter, I think, is the

144 WILLLIAM J. WOOD

course open to U.S. farmers in their present discontent. If they take radical action in their fight for genuine parity, they will be simultaneously exposing a strategic leverage point for getting at the forces that generate hunger as well as oppress the American farmer.

(5) Sustained Commitment

Probably the hardest part of being a change agent for an American is the need for perseverance. We are the "instant" society (instant breakfast, instant pudding, instant replay, instant weight-loss, instant service, instant coffee, instant intimacy, instant success). Someone has charged that the American approach to problems—from our forefathers' original flight from the oppressive societies of Europe, through the pioneering adventures ever seeking new frontiers, to the war in Vietnam—has been to seek the instant solution, the easy way out, running away from problems rather than seriously pursuing their solution.[31]

What I have observed in the food movement leads me to believe that, if such an analysis of our past is correct, we Americans are undergoing a profound change from our demand for instant solutions. We are becoming more reflective, more long-visioned, more patient.

Be that as it may, any strategy for significant change will demand sustained commitment. Hunger has been created through a long historical process. It won't be ended by a snap of the fingers. Because the disease of which hunger is a symptom is a systemic problem, the solution must be part of a historical process long enough to change systems.

Nor will all be success. The road to real victory will always be pockmarked by failures. Denis Goulet reminds us that "Vietnamese freedom fighters, the liberators of Guinea-Bissau, and struggling United States blacks all tell us that *victory comes to those who sustain their commitment even in the face of failure.*"[32] The strongest weapon in the campaign to transform the hunger-generating system will be perseverance in struggle. There is no easy or fast road to global justice.

IN SUM: If theology or ethics merely holds out lofty ideals and rests content with denouncing sinful structures, it will have no significant contribution to make toward the eradication of world hunger. An ethics will have prescriptive power only when it becomes an authentic *praxis.* It must not only point to the goals of food self-reliance and equitable control of productive resources. Nor is it enough, even, to specify the social and economic changes essential to the goals. It is further necessary to delineate concrete strategic measures to be taken for the required changes to come about.

I have suggested five indispensable components of an American strategy that would effectively contribute to the eradication of hunger: increased consciousness of individual and collective power; ongoing education and evaluation; collaboration and division of labor; exploiting the social forces and institutional leverage points that can best contribute to the desired change; and unflagging perseverance.

Conclusion

If Christians lived as Christians, there would not be any world hunger.[33] What we have to keep in mind, however, is that sin is still with us and will be until the Parousia. The essence of sin is blindness rather than malice, if I read the Gospels of John and Luke accurately, as well as my own reflective experience. The human race will be freed from that sin and its awful effects only through the cross of Jesus Christ—and through his resurrection and final coming. That's why the ones who do the most to transform this world are the prophets who resist power: Mother Teresa, Dorothy Day, Dom Helder Camara, Bishop Bernard Topel, Rutilio Grande, and many others whose names are not known. These are "the struggling deviants, the social prophets, who summon power to truth by their example of taking upon their shoulders the vulnerability of the oppressed."[34] They are living witnesses to the ultimate fact that the hope of which we are the bearers is based on the humble recognition of man's radical limitations and impotence; on our lack of trust in purely human and natural means to provide a global and lasting solution to today's problems.

But propelled to a great extent by the inspiration and prayers of the deviant prophets, the rest of us must continue to work at the nonheroic tasks. And we are capable, with all our limitations and foibles, of working together to change the structures that generate hunger, to build a more rational and equitable economic structure.

Notes

1. Institute for Food and Development Policy, 2588 Mission St., San Francisco, California 94110. Major work: *FOOD FIRST: Beyond the Myth of Scarcity* (Boston: Houghton Mifflin, 1977). I shall refer to other works throughout the paper.

2. Denis Goulet, "Beyond Moralism: Ethical Strategies in Global Development," in *Theology Confronts a Changing World* (The Annual Publication of the College Theology Society), Thomas M. McFadden, ed. (West Mystic, Conn.: Twenty-Third Publications, 1977).

3. "Undernutrition" means receiving too little food to lead a healthy, active life, while "malnutrition" connotes physiological impairment caused by a poor quality diet. Cf. *Agenda* (formerly *War On Hunger*), Vol. 1 No. 5 (May, 1978), p. 21.

4. *The Fourth FAO World Food Survey,* Food and Agriculture Organization of the United Nations (UNIPUB, Inc., 345 Park Avenue South, New York, N.Y. 10016, 1978).

5. For the kind of malnutrition that characterizes affluent Americans, see the devastating report prepared by the staff of the Select Committee on Nutrition and Human Needs, United States Senate, "Dietary Goals for the United States" (Washington, D.C.: U.S. Government Printing Office, Feb., 1977).

6. In Erich Fromm, "Introduction" to *Socialist Humanism: An International Symposium* (New York: Anchor Books, 1966), p. ix.

7. "What Can We Do About World Hunger?" I have paraphrased and adapted for my own purposes. This unpublished draft is not for quotation.

8. See Paul Barnett, "Tough Tomatoes," *The Progressive,* Vol. 41 No. 12 (December, 1977), pp. 32–37.

9. Figures supplied by *NUTRITION ACTION* (Center for Science in the Public Interest) in a promotional letter, November, 1977.

10. E. F. Schumacher, *Small Is Beautiful* (New York: Harper and Row Perennial Library, 1973), p. 293.

11. For a clear presentation of some historical ethical positions, see *Ethics for a Crowded World,* a seminar series prepared by the Center for Ethics and Social Policy, Graduate Theological Union, Berkeley, California, 1978.

12. From a 1978 Nestlé promotional brochure.

13. See, e.g., *Lifeboat Ethics,* George R. Lucas, Jr., and Thomas W. Ogletree (eds.) (New York: Harper Forum, 1976).

14. James V. Schall, *Welcome Number 4,000,000,000!* (Canfield, Ohio: Alba Books, 1977), p. 139.

15. W. Beckerman, "The Fallacy of Finite Resources," Social Survey (June, 1975), p. 146.

16. See the response of Lappé and Collins to Peter Huessy of the Environmental Fund: "Food First Revisited," *Ag World,* Vol. 4, No. 4 (April, 1978), pp. A–H.

17. Goulet, *op. cit.,* p. 29.

18. Pope Paul VI, Message to a Rural Life Conference (undated), NC news release quoted in *The Monitor* (Archdiocese of San Francisco), April 6, 1978.

19. Frances Moore Lappé and Joseph Collins, *World Hunger: Ten Myths* (San Francisco: Institute for Food and Development Policy, revised edition 1978), pp. 36–7. This is the first of a series of inexpensive booklets to be published by the Institute. Forthcoming publications include: "What Can I Do About World Hunger?" and "Food Self-Reliance."

20. Goulet, *op. cit.,* p. 13.

21. Marie Augusta Neal, *A SOCIO-THEOLOGY OF LETTING GO: The Role of A First World Church Facing Third World Peoples* (New York: Paulist Press. 1977).

22. Cf. Earthwork Calendar, May, 1978, "A Call To Farms," editorial (Center for Rural Studies, 3410 19th St., San Francisco, California 94110). One of the leaders in the farmers' strike is quoted as saying at a recent rally in Des Moines, "Just think, if Iowa farmers don't plant corn this spring, we're going to have a revolution in this country next fall."

23. Goulet, *op. cit.,* p. 34.

24. *FOOD FIRST* presents documented examples of peasant societies that have in fact overcome hunger, including the villagers of Kunjipukur in the Rangpur district of Bangladesh whose success encouraged over sixty other villages to take up the movement for self-reliance. During the 1974 famine when 80,000 to 100,000 people died of starvation in the Rangpur district, no one died of hunger in the self-reliant villages. These villages refused government assistance and collectively arranged for food contributions from anyone with a surplus. The food collected went to those without food, in exchange for work or other repayment collectively agreed upon. See pp. 392–398.

25. Peter Huessy, "Population Control or Food First," *Ag World,* Vol. 4 No. 1 (Jan., 1978), pp. 1–4; and Vol. 4 No. 2 (Feb., 1978), pp. 5–8. Deftly refuted by Lappé and Collins: Cf. note 16 above.

26. Jeremiah Novak, "A New Perception of World Hunger," *AMERICA,* Vol. 138, No. 18 (May 13, 1978), pp. 378–381.

27. Goulet, *op. cit.,* p. 23.

28. *Ibid.,* p. 27.

29. See Catherine Dunphy, "Canadians Fight Back Against Monopoly Agriculture," *New Internationalist,* No. 62 (April, 1978), p. 29.

30. Goulet, *loc. cit.*

31. See Philip Slater, *THE PURSUIT OF LONELINESS: American Culture at the Breaking Point* (Boston: Beacon Press, 1973).

32. Goulet, *loc. cit.* Emphasis added.

33. This is one of the themes of Ronald J. Sider's excellent book, *RICH CHRISTIANS IN AN AGE OF HUNGER: A Biblical Study* (New York: Paulist Press, 1977). This book provides a persuasive presentation of the biblical case against hunger. It makes a fine foundational introduction to Arthur Simon's *BREAD FOR THE WORLD* (New York: Paulist Press, 1975).

34. Goulet, *op. cit.,* p. 31.

Methodological Issues in the Ethics of Human Sexuality

Luke Salm

It is not my purpose to present yet another review of the controversial volume, *Human Sexuality*.[1] The first anniversary of the book's publication has already occasioned several reviews of the reviews.[2] Neither is it my intent to focus on specific issues in sexual ethics. I am satisfied that the publication of *Human Sexuality* has widened and advanced the discussion in this area. What is more satisfying is the extent to which the debate on sexuality has opened up and given concrete form to questions of system and method which have been under discussion for years in fundamental theological ethics. This aspect of the report and its implications is the focus of what is to follow.

Someone claims to have discovered an old Chinese curse: "May you live in a period of transition!" In the area of morality, the damnable part of living under such a curse, as we obviously do, is the plurality of options, presenting dilemmas at a fundamental level. In the transition from traditional moral theology to a contemporary theological ethics, there are prior decisions to be made about Bible and church authority, models, method, norms, absolutes and conflict situations. The different approaches to these questions and the variety of options have left some people with the impression that moral theology today is in a shambles. A more accurate assessment would locate the confusion in a failure to identify the options and make clear and consistent choices among them. For my present purpose I shall be talking about two types of fundamental questions. First I shall consider those that concern the function of extrinsic authority in theological ethics. Then I shall treat of options now available that are intrinsic to the work of systematic ethics at its various levels.

The first question of method concerns the authority of Bible and church. For some traditional-minded critics of *Human Sexuality,* all specific questions regarding sexual behavior have been resolved once and for all by the divine authority of Sacred Scripture and divine guidance given to the church. It is all summarized in one absolute norm: any directly willed sexual experience apart from the lawful use of marriage is objectively and intrinsically immoral.[3] In such a view of theological ethics, the only function of source analysis, empirical studies and systematic reasoning would be to refine and reinforce that norm.[4] Many of the most negative reactions to *Human Sexuality* have been based on this understanding of the task of a Catholic theologian.[5]

However, since Vatican II, and even before, new approaches to the function and method of theology have emerged within the Catholic theological community. Biblical and historical studies have undermined the force of many of the proof texts once invoked to support magisterial and theological positions. The notions of a perennial philosophy always and everywhere true, of a natural moral law unchanging and universally knowable, have been discarded or transcended. New areas of theological specialization, including many that demand competence in the physical and social sciences, have been identified and have become increasingly complex.[6] Distinctions have been made between the faith of the community and the formulation of that faith in doctrine, and between revealed truth and its propositional form in culturally conditioned sources.[7] The legitimacy of dissent, public and private, from non-infallible official teaching has been established;[8] this has been reinforced by historical studies that have brought to light instances of remarkable shifts and even positive errors in the official teaching that was imposed by church authority in the past.[9] Critical review of the councils from Nicaea to Vatican II show the extent to which official teaching is dependent on prior theological effort. Catholic theologians no longer work in isolation from one another or from their scholarly colleagues of other faiths.[10] In its traditional pursuit of an ever deepening understanding and systematization of our faith experience of the transcendent, theology can no longer content itself, if indeed it ever could, with simply repeating, explaining and defending church doctrine.

This creates a dilemma for revisionary studies such as *Human Sexuality* that in effect run contrary to the norm imposed by authority. The authors can accommodate presuppositions of the traditional method, arguing from biblical and church authority to support the revised norm. Or they can challenge the presuppositions of the traditional method, deny the relevance of the Bible and church authority in act-specific questions to argue for a revised norm based on intrinsic and systematic principles. Confusion results if a clear choice is not made between the two methods, if they are consciously or unconsciously adopted simultaneously in an attempt to have it both ways.

This objection could be leveled against *Human Sexuality*. The first chapter treats of sexuality in Scripture, the second of sexuality in church tradition. The same sequence is followed in the last chapter, which suggests guidelines for various forms of sexual behavior. The method is traditional but the conclusions are not. The function of the survey of Scripture and tradition is not clear. Sometimes these sources are treated as normative,[11] sometimes their significance is set aside by reason of their cultural conditioning.[12] Thus there is a conscious effort in Chapter IV to draw support from popes and councils for the principle upon which the theological argument is based.[13] Yet Chapter V gives pastoral and practical guidelines that diverge from norms established and reiterated by the same authority.[14] What seems to be lacking in the methodology is some principle to explain how the sources are used, what force the appeal to authority has, what the basis is for accepting its relevance in some aspects of the study but not in others.

The danger inherent in this ambiguity is that the sources begin to be treated selectively in what becomes in effect an apologetic for a particular theological position. Thus it may be legitimate to try to show, for example, that the story of Onan is not about onanism,[15] that the men of Sodom were not guilty of sodomy[16] or that Paul was opposed to prostitution but silent about pre-marital sex.[17] But the attempt fails if serious exegetical studies that support the traditional norm are passed over lightly or ignored, or if the impression is given that the Bible takes no stand on specific forms of sexual conduct. In the summary of church tradition much attention is paid to early church fathers and recent popes, but there is very superficial treatment of medieval scholasticism, Trent, the development of the manuals of moral theology and casuistry, probabilism, the neo-scholastic revival or the Modernist crisis, all of which did so much to forge the official norms.[18] This leaves the historical survey open to charges of selectivity and superficiality. It does little to allay suspicions of an attempt to have it both ways, looking to the tradition for support one moment and denying its relevance the next.

All these difficulties, evident not only in *Human Sexuality,* but in other published studies and in some academic courses as well, point to the central question of what is the function of religious authority in systematic ethics. Is the authority of Bible and church relevant to every aspect of all that falls under the broad umbrella of morality and ethics? Is that authority absolute or relative? Are there some aspects of the ethical enterprise where extrinsic authority has nothing definitive to contribute? Since the purpose of this paper is not simply to criticize the sexuality report but to address the methodological problems, it is important to make some response to these questions.

The authority of the Bible is absolute, of course, as long as one employs a fundamentalist exegesis, accepts a theory of verbal inspiration, or a concept of divine positive law based upon it, or confuses the divine revelation the Bible records with the words, images and literary forms used to convey it. That authority becomes relativized, however, not only partially but totally, once we accept principles of sound hermeneutics, a distinction between God's transcendent self-revelation and its culturally conditioned expression in the history of Israel and the early Christian community, the absoluteness of divine truth in comparison with our relative grasp of it, the expression of a lofty moral ideal held out to believers and the historical process by which the Judaeo-Christian tradition grows in its ability to realize the ideal in concrete forms of behavior. The moralist has a clear choice between naive supernaturalism and a sophisticated realization that revelation cannot simply be identified with its formulation in doctrine, myth and religious story. It is only in this way that we can justify revised norms for sexual behavior that do not agree literally with those of the community of Israel, the disciples of Jesus, or the primitive Christian church.

The approach to official church positions offers similar methodological options. Magisterial fundamentalism is at least as great a problem as biblical fundamentalism and the corresponding hermeneutical problems are equally complex. How God speaks to us in and through the church is as difficult to determine as how God speaks to us in and through the Bible. Catholics are expected to accept the doctrine that the church (and the pope) can teach infallibly in the area of morality. The historical fact is, that with regard to the morality of specific acts at least, it has never done so.[19] Either official positions on specific ethical questions are infallibly true or they are not. If they are not infallibly true, they are not absolute; they may develop and be revised (as they often have); dissent is possible and reasonable.[20] Since the right to dissent from authoritative

but non-infallible church pronouncements has been both theologi-
cally and legally established,[21] it is surprising that a study like *Human Sexuality* does not explicitly acknowledge that that is what it
is trying to do.

What is being advocated here is a relative autonomy for the rational and systematic aspect of the ethical enterprise that aims to
elaborate concrete norms for specific types of human behavior. This
is not the reductionist position that it may seem to be. Moral theologians have been saying for some time that the sources of revelation
do not provide information about specific ethical norms that are not
available outside the faith community.[22] Respect for a certain
autonomy in ethics is implicit also in the natural law tradition
which trusts the ability of human reason to discern God's will in an
ever more refined understanding of the created universe and of our
human nature. At one time it was thought that the sources of revelation as interpreted by church authority could provide norms for
judging conclusions of the physical and human sciences. Yet basic
theories of Copernicus, Galileo and Einstein, and some conclusions
of Marx, Durkheim and Freud in their respective fields, have been
recognized as valid independently, and often in contradiction of
church authority. The same could happen in ethics. It is incumbent
on the moral theologian to be clear about the function and limits of
religious authority in determining criteria for ethical behavior.

The claim for autonomy in some areas of systematic ethics does
not extend to the whole field of moral theology. Theological method
demands reference to faith and transcendence. Bible and church do
have something to say on moral issues.[23] Bible and church challenge the believer with standards of behavior which exceed the
norms that can be defended rationally in systematic ethics. The total love required by the Deuteronomic *mitzvah,* the "hard sayings"
of the Matthean Gospel or the perfection of the heavenly Father as
normative, and Paul's challenge to live by the Law of the Spirit are
obvious examples. Religion can set forth high ideals and powerful
motives to stimulate positive moral and ethical response in terms of
old or new covenant, love of God and neighbor, living in Christ, the
hope of a present and future reward. Religion has a prophetic function too, to point to sources of injustice and oppression, and expose
hypocrisy and sham.

Even within the elaboration of an ethical system, a religious
stance can provide breadth and balance. In the area of moral values
and absolutes a faith position can establish the importance of life,
love, fidelity, justice, and peace. Problems arise when religious au-

thority or beliefs are invoked to supply precise norms that are generally and transculturally valid in order to realize and maximize such values. In one view of theological method at least, it is here that religious authority might have to be set aside as inadequate and extrinsic to the business at hand.

This distinction between moral values and concrete ethical norms is basic to the problem of extrinsic authority in theological ethics. The authors of *Human Sexuality* are aware of this distinction and they appeal to it in the strictly theological part of their study.[24] But it is not explicitly and consistently invoked in those parts of the study that deal with the authority of Bible and church. It should be acknowledged that the sources themselves are not sensitive to the distinction. Religious authority can be as absolute in imposing specific concrete norms, especially in sexual ethics, as in affirming the most abstract and universal values. To distinguish between two levels of authority which the source documents clearly do not recognize is to misrepresent their intent. The distinction has to be established by the theologian, as the basis for a principle by which he can appeal to the sources to support the value structure of an ethical system while assuming personal responsibility for ethical reasoning used to elaborate a different set of norms. Unless some such principle is adopted the appeal to religious authority in moral theology will remain fraught with ambiguity and confusion.

A different kind of methodologial problem arises when we turn from external criteria derived from Bible and church authority to the criteria of systematic and rational ethics. In contemporary literature there seem to be four basic elements that comprise an ethical system, namely, stance, models, method and, ways of resolving conflict situations. Not all moralists give equal attention to each of these elements nor does everyone understand them in the same way. Many Catholic authors take positions on these elements that diverge significantly from the traditional Roman Catholic moral theology of the recent past. In the long run it is precisely new options available at the level of stance, models, method and conflict situations that have produced dissent from traditional Roman Catholic consensus on specific types of ethical behavior. This is especially true in the area of sexual ethics. It is not surprising, therefore, that moralists who have reviewed *Human Sexuality* have objected to it either because it by and large ignores the methodological debate, because it seems to opt for divergent methodologies simultaneously, or because some of its conclusions are based, implicitly or explicitly, on a methodological principle that the reviewer does not accept.[25]

For this reason, it might be worthwhile to review the various elements that constitute an ethical system, summarize the present state of the discussion and relate it to the quesions raised by the methodology of *Human Sexuality*.

First there is the question of stance. It is increasingly recognized in scientific disciplines of every kind that account must be taken of the presuppositions and predispositions of the practitioner, of the horizons or limits of the work (the objective pole) and of the attitude towards it (the subjective pole). Charles Curran seems to have imported this element into his moral theology from the ecumenical dialogue with Protestant colleagues on the nature of Christian ethics. The debate seems to center around which element or elements in the Christian faith are most relevant to the work of theological ethics. While most Protestant authors have opted for one such element—faith, for instance, love, or the person of Jesus Christ himself—Curran opts for five components of Christian belief with special emphasis on the reality of sin in balance with the goodness of creation, the eschatological promise that is ahead of us in balance with the embodied and incarnational dimension of Christian redemption that is operative in the here and now.[26] *Human Sexuality* would surely be found wanting, in terms of Curran's understanding of stance, for its failure to emphasize the sin element in many sexual situations where values conflict, for its failure to give due attention to the demonic element in human sexuality and the potential it has for exploitation and dehumanization. Not much attention is given to the nature of sin, the relation of sinful situation and sinful attitude to sinful acts, the current discussion on fundamental option and its implications for various forms of sexual behavior, or the interaction of objective and subjective factors in determining what constitutes serious violation of ethical norms. Other criticisms have been leveled at the report that could also be reduced to the matter of stance: the report is said to be overly optimistic, reflective of the naive attitude of celibates toward sex, too preoccupied with categories defined by the manualist tradition, too neglectful of the relation between sexual and social ethics.[27] All of this raises the interesting methodological question of what precisely is the function of stance in systematic ethics. Should stance enter directly into the process of ethical reasoning to provide criteria for judgment (as Curran seems to think); should it limit the scope of an ethical study (as the authors of the report seem to presume); or are the limitations of a stance that is too narrow in its horizons something to be overcome (as the critics of the report seem to imply)?

Some moralists skip over the question of stance and define the fundamental questions in terms of ethical models.[28] For them, the model provides the framework within which the ethical discussion takes place; it poses the most basic question that can be asked about human moral life and human behavior. From the time of the ancient Greeks the dominant ethical model has been teleological. In this model, ethical discourse begins by first raising the question of purpose, goals and means to an end. It considers human behavior as purposive and directed toward the good. Since the time of Kant an alternate approach has been to consider the basic, all-embracing first question as one of duty, control and law. It supposes that human behavior is governed by considerations of internal and external control; priority is given to the right rather than the good. The natural law model seems a combination of these two: insofar as it is based on observable purpose in nature it is teleological, insofar as it is law, a moral imperative "written in the heart," it is deontological. H. Richard Niebuhr has suggested a third model, that focuses on response-ability, as more basic and all-inclusive than purpose or duty. For him our human activity is characterized by our ability to respond to action upon us by interpreting what is going on and by being accountable to the expected response of others to our response. He outlines the patterns of response in our relation to others, to nature and events, to transcendence, to past, present and future and to the very contingency of our human existence.[29] Other moralists provide for these same elements within the framework of the traditional natural law, broadened to include those dimensions of human nature that stress its social, dynamic and relational aspects.[30] In all these models, the basic question concerns what it means to be human and to act in a human way. The model provides the framework for the first question to be asked about human behavior, not the answer or the norm. Thus within the teleological model, for example, opposite conclusions could be and have been reached on the morality of contraception depending on how one understands the purpose of sexual activity and marriage.

Human Sexuality seems to have generally ignored the contemporary discussion on ethical models. Like so many other studies that come from within the Catholic community, there seems to be a wavering back and forth between teleology and deontology, between purpose and moral imperative. The study might have been helped considerably in what it was trying to do by drawing on the potential of the responsibility model. In Niebuhr's analysis, we most often respond to physical nature (and presumably that includes our sexuality) by interpreting that nature through the interpretation of others.[31] In his insistence on accountability to the expectations of others, Niebuhr provides for both consistency and objectivity on the one hand and for gradual change and development on the other. The model avoids both the extremes of situationism and the rigid physicism of the traditional understanding of natural law. In locating the responsible self in a social context, the responsibility model has a unique potential to relate the personal dimension of sexual ethics, for example, to its evolving implications for social ethics. As a whole, the controversial study seems to be saying that believers and scientists in new social and cultural situations are beginning to interpret human sexuality differently; that it may be time to evolve a new, more suitable ethical response. A more explicit reference to the responsibility model could have provided an ideal framework to justify this position; the total argumentation and impact of the study would have been more consistent with itself and with a Christian understanding of what it is to be human.

Once a suitable stance has been taken and an appropriate ethical model chosen, the next step in a systematic ethics is to adopt an ethical method in the strict sense, that is, a rational process whereby conclusions are reached about what is normative behavior in specific areas of human activity. Most of the current discussion on method centers on norms, or middle axioms as they have been called,[32] that fall between the more universal and generally accepted moral values on the one hand and particular rules governing concrete situations on the other. Norms have as their function to protect and enhance values; they ought to be generally applicable, less absolute than the values themselves, and less open to revision than the rules.[33] Thus life is a value; the norm prohibits killing innocent people; a rule might require registration of hand guns.

A debate among ethicians today concerns whether the method by which we arrive at norms is primarily deductive, by way of logical reasoning from a priori first moral principles, or whether it is primarily inductive by way of an a posteriori analysis of the consequences of certain types of human behavior. Sometimes the deductive method is referred to as deontology and the inductive as teleology; this is confusing since these terms do not mean exactly the same thing in the discussion on method that they do when they refer to ethical models. The deductive method is criticized as abstract, rigid and impersonal; the inductive method is criticized for its utilitarian emphasis and for surrendering the ethical enterprise to the calculations of empirical science. Once again, the dominant trend among Catholic moralists today seems to combine the two approaches. The debate over situation ethics led some Catholic moralists to plead for greater attention in the formulation of ethical norms to human experience and the consequences of certain types of human behavior as analyzed by the empirical sciences.[34] In the discussion that followed, this methodology was refined to provide for reflection and judgment on the data in the light of values and preference principles. For this reason, this more inductive method favored by many contemporary Catholic moralists is known as modified consequentialism.[35]

Taken as a whole, *Human Sexuality* might seem to illustrate this approach. However, the authors are never very clear on the subject. The two crucial chapters of the study seem, in isolation, to illustrate the two extremes. Thus the analysis in Chapter III of the relevant data from the empirical sciences contains little that is evaluative; the chapter comes close to implying that what *is* determines what *ought to be,* that the descriptions of transcultural sexual behavior somehow provide the norms.[36] On the other hand, the theological development in Chapter IV begins by proposing a new definition of the nature of sexuality, one that is widely criticized for not being act-specific, and then proceeds from this a priori principle to draw conclusions about values and norms.[37] These two divergent methodologies are combined in Chapter V, which aims to give pastoral guidelines, in the light of the value principle of the total human person and his acts that was affirmed by Vatican II.[38] The methodological problem with this chapter is complicated by the review of the argument from authority, of Scripture and church tradition, with all the difficulties and ambiguities referred to earlier in this paper. This ambiguity of method results in a corresponding ambiguity of norms; the study seems content to affirm traditional values and question traditional norms without being very clear about how to formulate new ones or choose among available alternatives.

Related to the question of norms is the further methodological problem of absolutes and exceptions. How absolute are the norms and how do we provide for situations where values conflict? For centuries, Catholic moralists had only the principle of the double effect and the indirect voluntary to provide for exceptional cases. To this day, the norms imposed by the Roman authorities on abortion, sterilization and sexual ethics generally are all formulated in terms of direct and indirect.[39] In recent years, Catholic theologians have been trying to break away from the physicism of this approach.

Some appeal to the principle of proportionality that would justify what they call an ontic or pre-moral evil on the basis of a proportionate moral good that might be achieved.[40] Others simply appeal to the necessity for compromise by recognizing that sin is inevitable, that not all possible good can be achieved in every circumstance, that this justifies in certain situations of conflict exceptional actions that might ordinarily not be allowed.[41]

If there is one element more than any other that has led contemporary Catholic moralists to justify their dissent from official church teaching on specific moral questions, it is this challenge to the principle of the double effect and the absoluteness of the traditional norms. It is surprising, therefore, that the CTSA study which effectively dissents from the same teaching makes only passing reference to this discussion and its significance for sexual ethics.

Human Sexuality is not sufficiently explicit or consistent with regard to the options of stance, ethical models, methodology for elaborating ethical norms, and ways of providing for exceptions in conflict situations. The book affirms many positive values associated with sexuality, and there is analysis of various types of sexual behavior with some indication of how they are regarded by empirical science, religious authority and various schools of theological thought. But this is not enough to constitute a systematic study. The principal value of the book is descriptive; it has importance as a reflective survey; both its virtues and its faults have served to move forward the discussion both of sexual ethics and of methodology in theological ethics. One value it has for teachers of college theology is to illustrate the underlying importance of the neglected foundational questions. More explicit reference to options available at the foundational level might help students and the Catholic community generally to understand better the pluralism and dissent that characterize moral theology in a period of transition.

Notes

1. A. Kosnik et al., *Human Secuality: New Directions in American Catholic Thought* (New York: Paulist, 1977).
2. See R. McCormick, "Notes on Moral Theology" *Theological Studies* 39, 1 (Mar. 1978) 130–38; J. Gaffney, *"Human Sexuality:* A Review of Reviews" *Horizons* 5, 1 (Spring 1978) 81–85; D. Maguire *"Human Sexuality: The Book and the Epiphenomenon" CTSA Proceedings* 33 (1978).
3. See, e.g., H. Davis *Moral and Pastoral Theology,* vol. 2 (London: Sheed and Ward, 1936) p. 173. A brief survey of the theological and official

church positions can be found in J. Dedek, *Contemporary Sexual Morality* (New York: Sheed and Ward, 1971) pp. 31–39.

4. Thus in *Humani generis* Pius XII reaffirms the teaching of Pius IX that "the most noble office of theology is to show how a doctrine defined by the Church is contained in the sources of revelation" (NCWC transl. #21).

5. See the many instances cited in the survey of R. McCormick, "Notes . . ." in *TS* 39, 1 (*op. cit.*).

6. See especially Part Two of B. Lonergan, *Method in Theology* (New York: Herder and Herder, 1972).

7. The classic statement of this distinction was made by Pope John XXIII in his opening address of Oct. 11, 1962 to the Fathers of Vatican II. See the text in W. Abbot, *The Documents of Vatican II* (New York: America Press, 1966) p. 715. See the extended discussion in A. Dulles, *The Survival of Dogma* (Garden City: Doubleday, 1971).

8. C. Curran, *New Perspectives in Moral Theology* (Notre Dame: Fides, 1974) pp. 22–27. See also the discussion on theology and the magisterium in Chapters 5, 6 and 7 of A. Dulles, *Survival of Dogma (op. cit.)* and the survey in R. McCormick, "Notes on Moral Theology," *Theological Studies* 38, 1 (Mar. 1977) 84–100.

9. D. Maguire, "Moral Absolutes and the Magisterium" in C. Curran, *Absolutes in Moral Theology?* (Washington: Corpus, 1968), especially pp. 57–70.

10. This is especially true in the area of moral theology as attested by the recent involvement of Roman Catholics in the American Society of Christian Ethics. See C. Curran, *New Perspectives . . . (op. cit.)* p. 4 and *passim.*

11. Thus the report states: "Scripture provides us with certain fundamental themes as a basis on which to construct a modern theology of human sexuality" (*Human Sexuality,* p. 31). And again: ". . . we heartily endorse the recommendation of Vatican II that 'the nature of the human person and his acts' provides a basic principle from which to evaluate the morality of sexual behavior" (*Ibid.* p. 90).

12. Thus the report states: "As in the Old Testament, every statement in the New Testament regarding human sexuality is historically conditioned" (*Human Sexuality,* p. 30). Similar statements occur on pp. 17, 18, 40 and *passim.*

13. The reference is to *Gaudium et spes* (Abbott ed. #51) which states the principle that "the moral aspect of any procedure . . . must be determined by objective standards . . . based on the nature of the human person and his acts . . ." The last phrase is quoted in the chapter on tradition (*Human Sexuality* p. 48), again in the theological chapter (*Ibid.,* p. 90) and in the pastoral guidelines (p. 119). In none of these instances does the study note that the context presumes there is a question of conjugal love and demands adherence to the official doctrine on the methods of regulating procreation.

14. The divergence from official teaching is obvious and admitted in the treatment of the various forms of sexual behavior. This explains the exaggerated expressions of pastoral concern on the part of those who reject the report as an attempt to undermine church authority. See R. McCormick, "Notes . . ." in *TS* 39, 1 (*op. cit.*).

15. *Human Sexuality*, p. 15. Concerning the treatment of Scripture in the report, see G. Montague, "A Scriptural Response to the Report on Human Sexuality," *America* 137, 13 (Oct. 29, 1977) 284–85.

16. *Human Sexuality*, p. 191.

17. *Ibid.*, p. 154.

18. Thus in the twenty pages of this chapter of the report, six are devoted to the Fathers and eight to the modern popes with only two pages each to the early middle ages, the late middle ages and the modern period.

19. C. Curran, *New Perspectives* . . . (*op. cit.*), p. 22. See the discussion in D. Maguire, "Moral Absolutes . . ." (*op. cit.*); and more recently, J. Komonchak, "*Humanae Vitae* and its Reception: Ecclesiological Reflections," *Theological Studies* 39, 2 (June 1978). For the opposite view see J.C. Ford and G. Grisez, "Contraception and Infallibility" in the same issue of *TS.*

20. See fn. 8.

21. See fn. 9; also C. Curran and R. Hunt *et al., Dissent In and For the Church* (New York: Sheed and Ward, 1969).

22. See the discussion on creation and natural law in C. Curran, *New Perspectives* . . . (*op. cit.*) pp. 57–61: also on the social mission of the church, *Ibid.*, esp. pp. 155–56; also the survey of R. McCormick "Notes . . . ," *TS* 38, 1 (*op cit.*) 58–70

23. In addition to the discussions cited above, see J. Gustafson, *The Church as a Moral Decision Maker* (Philadelphia: Pilgrim Press, 1970).

24. *Human Sexuality* pp. 96–98.

25. See, for example, F. Meehan, "Love and Sexuality in Catholic Tradition" *America* 137, 11 (Oct. 15, 1977) 230–34; J. Farrelly, "An Introduction to a Discussion of 'Human Sexuality'," *CTSA Proceedings* 32 (1977).

26. C. Curran, *New Perspectives* . . . (*op. cit.*) pp. 47–86.

27. J. Wilcox, "Expanding the Debate on Human Sexuality" *Theta Alpha Kappa* 1, 1 (Spr. 1978), 55–57. See also, M. Neal "A Sociological Perspective on the Moral Issues of Sexuality Today," *Sexuality in Contemporary Catholicism* (New York: Seabury, 1976) pp. 61–70.

28. An extensive treatment of ethical models can be found in H.R. Niebuhr, *The Responsible Self* (New York: Harper and Row, 1963).

29. *Ibid.* Note the chapter headings: "Responsibility in Society," "The Responsible Self in Time and History," "Responsibility in Absolute Dependence."

30. See, for example, R. McCormick, "Human Significance and Christian Significance" in G. Outka and P. Ramsey *Norm and Context in Christian Ethics* (New York: Scribners, 1968) pp. 233–61, esp. pp. 239, 247–48;

see also Chapter 3 and 4 of J. Macquarrie, *Three Issues in Ethics* (New York: Harper and Row, 1970); Chapter 6 of I. Lepp *The Authentic Morality* (New York: Macmillan, 1965).

31. H.R. Niebuhr, *Responsible Self (op. cit.)* pp. 79–83.

32. J. Gustafson ascribes the term to J.H. Oldman as it is endorsed by J.C. Bennett; see J. Gustafson, "Context versus Principles: A Misplaced Debate in Christian Ethics," *New Theology No. 3* (New York: Macmillan, 1965) p. 85.

33. R. McCormick in his annual "Notes on Moral Theology" in *Theological Studies* is consistent in his application of this distinction.

34. J.G. Milhaven, "Objective Moral Evaluation of Consequences," *Theological Studies* 32, 3 (Sept. 1971) 407–30; see the critique of J. Connery, "Morality of Consequences: A Critical Appraisal" *Theological Studies* 34 (1973) 396–41; and the summary of C. Curran in Chapter 5 of *Themes in Fundamental Moral Theology* (Notre Dame, 1977) pp. 121–44.

35. R. McCormick in "Notes . . ." *TS* 38, 1 (Mar. 1977) p. 82 concurs with Curran on this description.

36. This is especially evident in the "Overview" and Conclusion of Chapter III of *Human Sexuality* pp. 56–60 and p. 77.

37. *Ibid.* pp. 80–88.

38. See fn. #13.

39. See the examples cited and the commentary in R. McCormick, "Sterilization and Theological Method" *Theological Studies* 37, 3 (Sept. 1976) 471–77. Other examples are cited and commented on by C. Curran in *New Perspectives . . . (op. cit.)* pp. 172 ff. pp. 196 ff.

40. This is well summarized by R. McCormick, "What the Silence Means: Richard A. McCormick Answers His Critics," *America* 129, 12 (Oct. 20, 1973) 290. For a consistent application of this principle to sexual ethics, see P. Keane, *Sexual Morality: A Catholic Perspective* (New York: Paulist, 1977).

41. This is the approach of N. Crotty, "Conscience and Conflict," *Theological Studies* 32, 2 (Jun. 1971) 208–32 and C. Curran in *New Perspectives . . . (op. cit.)*, e.g. pp. 191–92.

Play as an Ethical Paradigm for Sexual Intercourse

Mary Lou Grad

Within the tradition of Catholic sexual morality, ethical doctrine has recognized three major values in sexual intercourse, specifically, the unitive, the procreative, and the pleasuring. Of these
three values, the procreative has received primary emphasis. The
sexual union of a married couple has traditionally been thought to
reach its fruition in the establishment of a family. The procreation
and education of children was seen as the "primary" end of marriage, and the unitive and pleasuring values of the sexual union
were usually subordinated to their biological function.[1]

However, recent developments in sexual ethics have attempted
to integrate the importance of the various values of sexual intercourse, without limiting the prime value of sexual intercourse to its
biological dimension. The Second Vatican Council avoided making
the traditional distinction between primary and secondary ends of
marriage.[2] The recent report, *Human Sexuality: New Directions in
Catholic Thought,* considers married life-styles other than those
that include children.[3]

Speaking of the "unique possibilities" offered in marriage in
comparison with other love relationships, Philip Keane explains
that marriage provides the ambience most favorable for the birth
and education of children; and for this reason, children can be
viewed as "the primary end of marriage."[4] Keane adds however
that if marriage is too quickly defined by children, other values "essential" to marriage may be negated.[5]

Andrew Greeley recently commented that the reevaluation of
traditional sexual norms is not a result of change in fundamental
principles, but rather a result of the changing circumstances in

162

which these principles are applied and the new insights gained by the social sciences into human behavior.[6] Research into the disciplines of theology, psychology, sociology, and particulaly the reflection of married couples on the significance of sexual intercourse has provided valuable insights and data that need to be considered in the formulation of paradigms for sexual ethics.

This article is an attempt to exploit the concept of "play," expounded by Hugo Rahner, as an ethical paradigm for sexual intercourse. The concept of play will be examined as presented in Rahner's book, *Man at Play*. The term "sexual intercourse," in this article, will be limited to sexual genital intercourse. This limitation of the term is for the purpose of precision and is not intended to negate the dimensions of sexual intercourse that extend beyond genital activity. The article will include: first, an evaluation of a foundation for a system of ethics; secondly, a working definition of the term "ethical paradigm"; thirdly, a definition of play, as presented by Rahner; fourthly, a summary of the key principles of Rahner's theology of play; and lastly, a proposed delineation of play as an ethical paradigm for sexual intercourse.

A Foundation of Ethics

A system of ethics must recognize human beings in the situation of their created existence. Human personality is a composite of three fundamental dimensions—the biological, the psycho-sociological, and the transcendent. A human being is capable of reflection on his own activities. A human life-style is a composite of various modes of behavior, not only those that are freely chosen but also those that are strongly influenced by social norms or peer pressure. The transcendent dimension enables human beings to respond to an Otherness that transcends their created, earthly existence.

In the exercise of these three dimensions of personality, man finds an inner-connectedness. An imbalance of the psycho-social dimension often affects the functioning of an individual on the physical level, as in psychosomatic illness. A personal affirmation or negation of the transcendent dimension may determine behavior on the psycho-social levels, as may an attitude of faith or nihilism. Man is not disincarnated spirit or a spiritless body. In the formulation of an ethical paradigm for sexual intercourse, man must be viewed under all three aspects of human personality—the biological, the psycho-sociological, and the transcendent. Their totality represents the primal integration of the human personality, an integration that should be the goal of any ethical system.

Ethical Paradigm

A system of ethics emphasizes the importance of accepting personal responsibility for the fullest development of one's own life and potential within the context of created existence, and affirming the same dignity of life for others. Within the Christian context, such affirmation is based on a recognition of man as the created image of God. An ethical paradigm is a rule of conduct or mode of response—physical, psycho-sociological, and transcendent—to a situation in which one concretizes a moral value. An ethical paradigm "must respect the contingent while maintaining an awareness of perfection."[7]

An ethical paradigm for sexual morality must encompass an active endeavor to realize the primal integrity of the three dimensions of the human personality. At the same time, the ethical paradigm must possess a flexibility for its development through a dialectical interaction between the values of an ethical paradigm and its praxis.

The primal integrity of the human personality is not affirmed by negating the exercise of sexual genital activity, but rather in integrating this activity into the total dimension of interpersonal relationships. Such affirmation and integration lead to a recognition of man and woman in their primal integrity as created images of God—male and female.

The flexibility of a satisfactory ethical paradigm promotes the integration of the value of the principle with its praxis. Abstraction of a value from an ethical paradigm that negates praxis represents an ethical modality that denies the basic integrity of the human personality in interpersonal relationships. On the other hand, praxis must never be the sole norm for moral behavior.

Theology of Play: Rahner's Definition

Hugo Rahner, in his book *Man at Play* posits three fundamental principles: first, the *deus ludens*—the God who plays—ontologically defines man as the *homo ludens*—the man who plays; secondly, the "grave-merry" man—the one who seeks a balance between the joy and tragedy of human existence—is the modality of personality expressed by the *homo ludens;* and thirdly, *eutrapelia*—a recognition of the transcendent dimension in human activity—is the virtuous expression of the *homo ludens*.

Play, as defined by Rahner, symbolizes the integration of the three dimensions of the human personality:

> For play is a human activity, which engages of necessity both soul and body. It is the expression of an inward spiritual skill successfully realized with the aid of physically visible gesture, audible sound and tangible matter. As such, it is precisely the process whereby the spirit "plays itself into" the body of which it is a part.[8]

It is Rahner's integration of physical, psychological, and transcendent dimensions of the human personality, in his definition of play, that enables the concept of play to be considered as an ethical paradigm for sexual intercourse. The physical act of sexual intercourse can be one of the deepest expressions of the spiritual union. Rahner concludes, in his definition of play, that the physically visible act becomes an "expression of an inner fullness that is sufficient to itself."[9]

Principles of Rahner's Theology of Play

Deus Ludens

Rahner derives the concept of the *deus ludens*—the God who plays—from the creative activity of God. Rahner explains that God's creativity is not a metaphysical constituent of his nature, but rather emanates from his freedom. This creative activity of God has the character of a "most profound" meaning, but is not a metaphysical necessity—God's creative activity is "meaningful but not necessary."[10]

Rahner uses the writings of Plato, Philo of Alexandria, Holy Scripture, and Gregory of Nazianzen to illustrate that the concept of the creative activity of the *deus ludens*—"meaningful but not necessary"—has been experienced and expressed throughout history.

Plato, in his teachings, defined man as a "plaything in the hand of God."[11] Plato explains that man was ordained to his end by the God who created him, and therefore man's life could only be understood if the transcendent dimension of his existence was considered. In his excursus on human nature in the *Laws*, Plato explains that the man who plays has found a mean "between the tragedy of existence and the light-hearted surrender to the game of life ... which is, mysteriously guided by the goodness of a Wisdom also at play."[12]

Rahner cites Philo of Alexandria's use of Heraclitus' idea of the nature of flux in all things to describe the rise and fall of empires, all of which are ordered by the divine and playing Logos.[13] This divine and playing Logos makes the things of the world intelligible, even creating a balance of justice within the empires of man.

Rahner also cites Scripture's mention of the same divinely ordering creative freedom in the Hebrew concept of *Hochmah*—divine Wisdom "playing before the face of the world-creating God."[14] It is this playfulness of Wisdom which is spoken of in Proverbs:

When he fixed the heavens firm, I was there ... When he laid down the foundations of the earth, I was by his side, a master craftsman, delighting him day after day.[15]

Gregory of Nazianzen in his *Carmina* illustrates the prevalence of the concept of the playing Logos in the writings of the Greek Fathers of the Church:

For the Logos on high plays, stirring the whole cosmos back and forth, as he wills into shapes of every kind.[16]

Thus, the *deus ludens,* whose creative activity is "meaningful but not necessary," orders and makes intelligible man's created existence. This meaningful creative activity can be seen most vividly in the covenantal relationship in which God offers the world to man, with man in the role of co-creator. The covenant of God with man presupposes a creation given order by the Transcendent. The "gift" of the covenant implies the necessity of man not only to recognize that order but also to bring it to fruition as co-creator.

Grave–Merry Man

The response of the *homo ludens*—the man who plays—to the creative activity of God, is defined by Rahner as the "grave-merry" man. Rahner borrows this term from the untranslatable Greek phrase *anèr spoudogéloios.*[17] The *homo ludens,* according to Rahner, is continually aware of the joyfulness and the tragedy of earthly existence.[18] Human existence is joyful because it is securely rooted in God. The tragedy of human existence results from man's abuse of freedom. The "grave-merry' man lives in earnest but realizes the insufficiency of his earthly existence; he does not live the extremes of frivolity or despair.[19] He acknowledges the transcendent dimension of existence and the "gift" of the created earthly order but recognizes his frequent inability to integrate this dimension existing not in a polarization but rather in a creative tension.

Eutrapelia

In his search for the integrity of the earthly and transcendent dimensions of his existence, the "grave-merry" man exercises the virtue of *eutrapelia*. This virtue appears in the fourth book of Aristotle's *Nicomachean Ethics*. Aristotle used the term *eutrapelos*—literally translated as "well-turning"—to describe a person who stood between the extreme of *homolochos*—the "buffoon," and *agoikas*—the "boor."[20] The mature person who practiced the virtue of *eutrapelia*, according to Aristotle, possessed a "mobility" of soul. This capacity allowed the person to focus toward "relaxing things" without becoming engulfed by them. The object of *eutrapelia* is "play for the sake of seriousness." Aristotle described amusement as a form of rest from work activity.[21]

However, the virtue of *eutrapelia* did not find a place in the morality of early Christianity. The term *eutrapelos* had taken on the connotation of a person who was a "garrulous windbag."[22] Paul warned the early Christians in the Epistle to the Ephesians (5:4) to avoid salacious talk.[23] Norms for Christian behavior deterred the Christian from behaving in a manner contrary to the seriousness with which the Christian should approach the world.

Aquinas, in his commentary on the *Nicomachean Ethics*, introduced *eutrapelia* into Christian morality. Aquinas interpreted Aristotle's concept of moderation in play to mean that play was acceptable for the Christian because it provided mental relaxation.[24] Just as a man needed rest from physical labor, he also required rest from mental labor. Aquinas further developed the explanation of *eutrapelia* to describe a virtue with which a person created a balance between the comic and the serious and recognized the proper place and proper time for each.[25]

The virtue of *eutrapelia*, as a moral expression of play, implies the capacity of a person to "transform" the elements of creation by viewing them in the proper order of creation. *Eutrapelia* restores order for one who has disintegrated the basic integrity of man by restoring balance between the transcendent and earthly dimensions of human existence.

Application of Principles to Sexual Ethics

Deus Ludens

The creative activity of the *deus ludens* manifests itself most vividly in the creation of man and woman and in the covenantal relationship that God enacts with them. The creative activity of God prior to man's creation did not possess the totality of the biological, psychological, and transcendent dimensions of the human personality. Man alone found no complement for his human personality. The exclamation of man—"This at last is bone from my bone, and flesh from my flesh!"—perfectly conveys his enthusiastic response to the discovery of a "soul-mate."[26] The creation of woman enabled man to experience a fellowship that involved all dimensions of his personality.

The covenantal relationship that God establishes with man is reflected in the intimate character of the fellowship between man and woman. Within the context of the Old Testament, Cornelius Van der Poel has distinguished four basic covenants in which God has revealed himself to man: 1) the covenant in Paradise, 2) the Noahite covenant, 3) the covenant with Abraham, and 4) the covenant on Sinai.[27] The fullness of these covenants is revealed in the person of Jesus Christ. Within the expression of these five covenants, God continually manifested himself in an increasingly intimate relationship with man.

The covenantal relationship of man and woman, traditionally expressed in the institution of marriage, mirrors the *deus ludens* by its image of the intimate relationship and the "giftness" of the partners to each other. Although the individual in society exists in a variety of relationships, the intimate relationship of a marital union is not only unique but can be considered as "gift"; not all people who would like to enter such a relationship can find a suitable partner. It can be concluded from Rahner's description of the creative activity of the *deus ludens* as "meaningful but not necessary" that the fellowship of the covenantal relationship is "meaningful but not necessary."

The affirmation of marriage in the Old Testament is best understood in the context of Yahweh's relationship with Israel. The language, used in the Old Testament to describe the intimate relationship between God and his people, is drawn from human experience. Whenever the connection between human marriage and the covenant is established in the texts of the Old Testament, it is the saving covenant itself that is at issue.[28]

In the New Testament, the covenantal relationship is expressed in the image of the union between Christ and his Church. The love binding Christ to his Church is an expression of the love binding Yahweh to Israel in the covenant. Paul refers to the covenantal relationship when he states that:

> A man never hates his own body, but feeds it and looks after it; and that is the way Christ treats the church ... For this reason, a man must leave his father and mother and be joined to his wife, and the two will become one body.[29]

The covenantal relationship of God with man expresses the cosmic order of reality—the creative activity of the *deus ludens*. The covenant that a man and a woman enact with each other is a self-disclosure, going beyond ego, imaging the covenant of God with man. As God continually expressed himself in a more intimate relationship with his people in a free self-disclosure, each partner in a covenantal relationship works to enhance an ambience of intimacy in which self-disclosure can be effected.

"Grave-Merry Man"

It was previously noted that the modality of response of the *homo ludens* to the creative activity of God is the "grave-merry" man. The "grave-merry" man comprehends reality beyond its sense impressions and is always ready to integrate the earthly and transcendent dimensions of human existence. The "grave-merry" man is aware of the tension between the joyfulness and the tragedy of human existence.

Within the context of a sexual ethic the *homo ludens*, through the posture of the "grave-merry" man, attempts to recognize the inherent value within the acts of sexual intercourse—the sharing of an intimate relationship, the propagation of the species, and the intense physical pleasure. The "grave-merry" man is also cognizant that tragic consequences can result from the abuse of sexual intercourse, disintegrating basic dimensions of the human personality. Such abuse either gives priority to the physical pleasure or negates

the physical pleasure for a desire to achieve a superior, spiritual relationship. The "grave-merry" man is conscious of the need for creative tension among the three dimensions of human personality.

Within the context of reproduction, the "grave-merry" man
would extend the dimensions of creative intimacy beyond biological
reproduction to include the psychological and transcendent spheres
of the partners' personalities. Robert and Mary Joyce, in *New Dynamics in Sexual Love,* distinguish these two dimensions of human
reproduction by using the phrases: "quantitative" reproduction—
resulting in the procreation of a third person, the child; and "quali-
tative" reproduction—which promotes social values and the development of the partners themselves within an ambience of unconditional love.[30] This distinction in reference to creative intimacy
incorporates the biological, psychological, and transcendent dimensions of each partner, thus restoring a primal integration in their
personalities as created images of God.

Eutrapelia

The virtue of *eutrapelia,* as described by Rahner, not only enables man to comprehend the ontological order of his created existence but also to recognize the ontological dimension of the human
activities in which he is engaged. Recognition of the transcendent
dimension enables man to sacralize or sacramentalize the human
reality of created existence in its relation to the transcendent, thus
integrating reality into its proper created order. The covenantal relationship of marriage embodies the ontological reality of the transcendent covenant of God with man, the reality of the individual
personalities, and the physical act of intercourse. Andrew Greeley
has explained that "sex is one of the best sacraments (re-presenta-
tions) of the love of God for his people, precisely because of the
built-in tendency towards commitment involved in sexual love."[31]
Such a commitment is a free self-donation of each partner to the
other with a witness of fidelity to the relationship. This commitment mirrors the fidelity expressed in God's covenant with Israel.

The act of sexual intercourse is a meaning-giving dialectical act
in which the substantive love of the covenantal relationship finds
expression through affectionate acts of the body. The intensity of
communion experienced emotionally, physically, and transcenden-
tally at the moment of orgasm presents an opportunity for immediate integration of the three corresponding dimensions of the human
personality of each partner. Sexual intercourse becomes a meaning-
giving act inasmuch as it expresses the quality of the relationship

at the psychological and transcendent levels. Within the context of the sacrament of marriage, the sexual genital act, in fact, consummates the marriage. Speaking of the need for intercourse, John B. Gruenenfelder has explained that:

> the psychological need for intercourse witnesses to the ontological union. The psychological need is not simply because of the physical pleasure; but because the marital act expresses and bonds the union, commemorates the union and is an ontological union itself.[32]

Conclusion

Play, as an ethical paradigm, is most vividly manifested in the expression of genital sexual intercourse.[33] The partner in the covenantal relationship is presented with the possibility of recognizing the physical act as an image of the ontological reality of God's covenant relationship with man.

The principal concepts of Rahner's theology of play—the *deus ludens,* the grave-merry man, and *eutrapelia*—as applied to sexual intercourse, present a model of intimacy in which the physical, psycho-sociological and transcendent dimensions of the human personality can find a complete ontological integration. Rahner's concept of the *homo ludens* mirrors the covenantal relationship of *deus ludens* with man—meaningful but not necessary. The posture of the grave-merry man prohibits the sexual act from giving priority to one particular value of intercourse to the denial of others. The virtue of *eutrapelia* enables the partners in a conjugal relationship to see the transcendent dimension of their unconditional love. Play as an ethical paradigm for sexual intercourse achieves the goal of the primal integration of man as the created image of God.

Notes

1. Charles Curran, *Themes in Fundamental Moral Theology* (Notre Dame: University of Notre Dame Press, 1977), p. 167. Curran explains that, according to Ulpian, the "procreation and education of children is the classical example of natural law which is common to man and animals." The human dimension of reproduction is an addition to the primary dimension of animality. Curran further explains that the dimensions of "relationality" and "love" were relegated to the secondary ends of intercourse since they were not constitutive of animal sexuality.

2. *Gaudium et Spes* in *Documents of Vatican II,* ed. Walter Abbott, S.J. (New York: America and Association Press, 1966), n. 48b. The Council also avoided using the terminology of "primary" and "secondary" ends in n. 50.

3. Anthony Kosnik, *et al., Human Sexuality: New Directions in Catholic Thought* (New York: Paulist Press, 1977), pp. 140–43.

4. Philip Keane, S.S., *Sexual Morality: A Catholic Perspective* (New York: Paulist Press, 1977) ch. 6, n. 6, p. 208.

5. *Ibid.,* p. 96.

6. Andrew Greeley, "Moral Choices in Contemporary Society: The Dilemmas of Sex," *National Catholic Reporter,* Vol. 13 (February 4, 1977), p. 15.

7. Eric Osborn, *Ethical Patterns in Early Christian Thought* (New York: Cambridge University Press, 1976), pp. 4–5.

8. Hugo Rahner, *Man at Play* (New York: Herder & Herder, 1972), p. 6. (hereafter cited as MP).

9. *Ibid.,* p. 7.

10. *Ibid.,* p. 11.

11. Plato, *Laws,* 803 B.C., cited by Hugo Rahner, *MP,* p. 11.

12. *Ibid.,* pp. 13–14.

13. Philo, *Quod Deus sit Immutabilis,* 172–6 ed. Cohn-Wendland, II, p. 92 11. 5–23, cited by Rahner, *MP,* p. 15.

14. Rahner, *MP,* p. 19.

15. Proverbs, 8:27–31, cited by Rahner, *MP,* p. 19.

16. Gregory Nazianzen, *Carmina,* I,2,2, vv. 589–90 (PG 37, 624A f.), cited by Rahner, *MP,* p. 23.

17. Rahner, *MP,* p. 27.

18. *Ibid.,* pp. 26–27.

19. *Ibid.*

20. Aristotle, *Nicomachean Ethics,* IV, 14 (1128a.), cited by Rahner, *MP,* pp. 93–94.

21. *Ibid.,* X, 6 (1176b), cited by Rahner, *MP,* pp. 94–95.

22. Rahner, *MP,* pp. 95–96.

23. Ephesians, cited by Rahner, *MP,* p. 96.

24. Aquinas, Saint Thomas, *Summa Theologica,* II–II q. 168 a.2, cited by Rahner, *MP,* p. 100.

25. *Ibid.*

26. Pierre Grelot, *Man and Wife in Scripture* (New York: Herder & Herder, 1964), p. 35.

27. Cornelius Van der Poel, "The Search for Human Values," A lecture in moral theology at Duquesne University, Pittsburgh, Summer, 1973. The four covenants which Van der Poel explicates are: 1) the Covenant in Paradise in which God reveals himself as Creator (Gn. 1:28–31), 2) the Noahite Covenant in which God revealed himself as Master Avenger and the Merciful One (Gn. 9:3), 3) the Covenant with Abraham in which God re-

vealed himself to various cultures (Gn. 17), and 4) the Covenant of Sinai in which God manifests his presence to one particular culture (Ex. 34:1–28). Each covenant manifests a growing degree of intimacy in God's relationship with man.

28. Edward Schillebeeckx, O. P., *Marriage: Human Reality and Saving Mystery* (New York: Sheed and Ward, 1965), p. 31.

29. Ephesians, 5:29–32, cited by Rahner, *MP,* p. 96.

30. Robert and Mary Joyce, *New Dynamics in Sexual Love* (Collegeville: St. John's University Press, 1970), p. 62.

31. Greeley, "Moral Choices in Contemporary Society: The Dilemmas of Sex," p. 15.

32. John B. Gruenenfelder, "The Unity of the Marital Act," in *Sex: Thoughts for Contemporary Christians,* ed. Michael Taylor (New York: Doubleday & Company, 1972), p. 107.

33. Gruenenfelder reiterates Rahner's definition of play as the "Physically visible gesture ... whereby the spirit plays itself into" the body of which it is a part.

A Note on the Authors

SILVIO E. FITTIPALDI is chairman of the Religious Studies Department of Villanova University.

MARY LOU GRAD MLECKO is a mental health therapist at the Indiana County Guidance Center, Indiana, Pennsylvania.

THADDEUS J. GURDAK teaches in the Department of Religion at West Virginia Wesleyan College.

ALBERT A. HIEBERT is academic dean at Winnipeg Bible College, Otterburne, Manitoba.

RODERICK HINDERY teaches religion and social ethics at Temple University.

LEANDER E. KECK is dean of the Divinity School of Yale University.

PAUL J. PHILIBERT, O.P. is a member of the Boys Town Center and teaches in the Department of Religion and Religious Education at the Catholic University of America.

LUKE SALM, F.S.C. teaches in the Department of Religious Studies at Manhattan College.

S. YOUREE WATSON, S.J. teaches philosophy at the Center for Jesuit Formation at Loyola University in New Orleans.